THE DREAM, THE JOURNEY, ETERNITY, AND GOD

ALSO BY SARA LANDON

*The Wisdom of The Council: Channeled Messages for Living Your Purpose**

ALSO BY MIKE DOOLEY

*A Beginner's Guide to the Universe**

An Adventurer's Guide to the Jungles of Time and Space

*Channeled Messages from Deep Space (with Tracy Farquhar)**

Choose Them Wisely: Thoughts Become Things!

Dreams Come True: All They Need Is You

Infinite Possibilities

Leveraging the Universe

*Life on Earth**

Manifesting Change

*Notes from the Universe Coloring Book**

*Playing the Matrix**

The Complete Notes from the Universe

*The Top 10 Things Dead People Want to Tell YOU**

Totally Unique Thoughts

Your Magical Life

*Available from Hay House
All of the above are available at your local bookstore,
or may be ordered by visiting:

Hay House USA: www.hayhouse.com®
Hay House Australia: www.hayhouse.com.au
Hay House UK: www.hayhouse.co.uk
Hay House India: www.hayhouse.co.in

THE DREAM, THE JOURNEY, ETERNITY, AND GOD

Channeled Answers to Life's Deepest Questions

SARA LANDON

AND

MIKE DOOLEY

HAY HOUSE

HAY HOUSE INDIA

New Delhi • London • Sydney

Carlsbad, California • New York City

Published in the United States by: Hay House, Inc.: www.hayhouse.com®
Published in Australia by: Hay House Australia Pty. Ltd.: www.hayhouse.com.au
Published in the United Kingdom by: Hay House UK, Ltd.: www.hayhouse.co.uk
Published in India by: Hay House Publishers India: www.hayhouse.co.in

Project editor: Anna Cooperberg
Freelance Editor: Lynn Komlenic
Cover design: Barbara LeVan Fisher
Interior design: Bryn Starr Best

First Hay House India Edition 2024

ISBN: 978-81-19554-82-9

Printed at Repro India Limited

Dedicated to those now awakening.

CONTENTS

Introduction

BY MIKE DOOLEY

I'll never forget December 2019. I was finally reading Paramahansa Yogananda's *Autobiography of a Yogi* after being advised by many to do so for at least two decades. Until that point in my life I hadn't been much of a reader, but this book and the COVID sequestration that immediately followed changed everything. Its implications for living a far richer, supernatural, more miraculous life were absolutely thrilling. I'd always suspected as much, but had never, ever imagined it could be our reality—my reality. Since then, I've ravenously consumed all else I could find on the topic of self-realization.

Back to December 2019. As I was deep into *Yogi*, a new acquaintance, Sara Landon, offered me a private, channeled session with The Council—a wise contingent of ascended masters who claim to be "future" versions of ourselves. The serendipitous timing of what The Council shared with me—some of which is included later in this volume—the content of which echoed exactly what I was reading, and feeling, still makes my head spin in near disbelief. It was like a date with destiny.

I've come to learn through The Council, and by now many others, that I'm not alone. Either in desire or readiness, to grow like we have never grown. This is the precise time on planet Earth foreseen by sages and ancient prophecy makers for this exact planetary awakening, complete with geological upheaval, atmospheric catastrophes, and above all, resistance and polarization of the masses, like the proverbial wheat being separated from the chaff. Not a separation overseen by a biblical judge, however, but one determined by whether each of us chooses to be moved more by love or fear.

It didn't take long for me and Sara to realize it would be fun to work together with our respective spiritually minded audiences, so we hosted a free online workshop of the same title as this book. We wanted to test the waters of appeal and marketability for our brand of "awakening within the dream of life." Twenty-five thousand viewers gave an enthusiastic "Yes!" It was electrifying.

Now, it's your turn.

You hold in your hands a book that was meant to reach you at exactly this time in your journey, to remind you of who you really are and of the ease, peace, love, and happiness that imminently await your recognition. You are of the divine, by the divine, and here for the divine—pure Source Energy. The eyes and the ears of God almighty come alive in the dream of life, destined to consciously realize this for yourself and to live like you have never even imagined.

We've waited a long time for this, you and I. To command the elements, creatively fulfilled, loving our lives, with cups so overflowing that our burning desires begin shifting outward to help others see and live the truths that have made our lives so extraordinary. We'll thereby help to usher in a golden age unlike any in recorded history, as legions now excitedly watch in the unseen, as anxious for us to join them in awareness as they are to join us in the flesh.

May you find in these pages answers to all of your questions, and far more. May they trigger and confirm your own inner suspicions of life's glory and your power. I have every confidence that herein, as we pilgrimage through these sacred jungles of time and space—just as planned, so long ago, back at the beginning of time—you'll find the confirmation, validation, and inspiration you need to go any distance you desire.

Yours in the adventure,

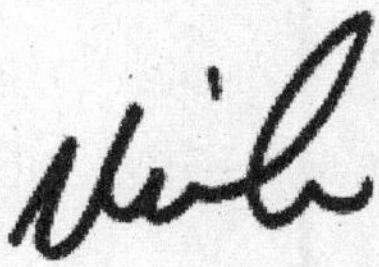

SECTION 1

Who Is The Council?

In this section, The Council answers questions about channeling, higher wisdom, remembering who you really are, and why they are here with us at this important time in human evolution.

We are so pleased and delighted to have the opportunity to speak with you, our dear friend, on this fine and glorious day indeed. We wish to tell you first that while our words to you are important, this is a vibrational experience of remembering who you really are, why you are here, and all that you intended when you chose this magnificent life experience. Because we assure you, *life is meant to be so very good for all of you!*

Thank you so much. Would you share a few opening words with us, and then for the benefit of our readers, tell us who you are and what realm or dimension you're coming from? Many of us are familiar with the channeled entities or collectives known as Seth, Ramtha, Abraham, Edgar Cayce. Are you like them? Have you had former lifetimes here on earth?

We could not be more excited to be here with you to answer your questions and to co-create in formless and in form this magnificent manifestation.

We will begin with your first question, "Who are you?" Simply put, we are a collective of ascended master beings with a higher level of consciousness and a grander perspective of the human experience.

It is our great love for humanity, the planet, and this human experience that focuses us into an awareness in which we are available to you. We come through Sara because of her asking, but we are also available to all.

We came forth because we promised we would, and we are here to remind you of your own wisdom, which you never intended to forget. It might be difficult for your "human"[1] to comprehend, but you are us—ascended master beings, every single one of you, who've focused yourself into the human experience to be on the planet at this time. You're here for the expansion of your soul, for the expansion of consciousness. You're here to express yourselves and to have the experiences you want to have as you explore, play, and create.

Whenever you're reading this, we assure you, we promise you, you drew this conversation to you at this time so that you could remember. You're ready to remember. There are so many of you on the planet at this time who came here to awaken to the truth of who you are and to come into the realization of your true spiritual nature, where you can then begin living as the masters you are—fully embodied, fully enlightened, fully living in ascended states of consciousness *while in physical form* on this planet, Heaven on Earth.

---

[1] The Council refers to the awareness we have of ourselves, our human side, as "your human," to distinguish this aspect of our experience from all else that we truly are, throughout and beyond space and time.

Our highest answer to "Who are you?" is: We are you; you are us. We are the higher selves of every one of you. We are here to be a light along the way so that you can more easily come into greater levels of awareness and consciousness, with a higher perspective of the human experience.

All of this is possible for you.

We are always with you, we are always available to you, never separate from you, and that is why for so many of you this will be a feeling of coming home to the truth within you.

I feel the truth of this whenever I speak with you.

Indeed. To embody the knowing that you are ascended master beings on the planet is so important. You're here of your own choosing in part because of the elevation, expansion, and transformation of consciousness that's happening on the planet at this time. You are so very important. And while everything is perfect and everything will unfold in divine perfect time, there is a far greater purpose for Earth in this vast and glorious universe as humanity elevates its collective consciousness.

The dream, the journey, eternity, and God are also things you never intended to forget. There's a dream within your heart that knows that peace, joy, love, harmony, well-being, and freedom is your divine, inherent birthright. This is who you really are and why you're here. You remember and come into this realization, and create your individual and collective realities the way you wish them to be, you'll realize you were each dreaming the same dream all along.

We could not be more excited for you at this time where you can live in a state of consciousness that you call

Heaven on Earth or a New Earth. It is here for you now. It is available to each of you. There is something within you that knows—that remembers—that it's possible for you. Allow it in. Allow it in. Allow it in. And as you read this again and again and again, you will hear more every time.

You also asked us from where we come, how we compare to your other beloved teachers, and if we have had human experiences.

First, you are now having a human experience in the 3rd Dimension. A dimension of consciousness characterized by separation, in which you experience being apart from or disconnected from all else. A common experience for many there is to perceive things in polarities—good or bad, right or wrong. It's also common to think that you are just your body, and anything that is not your body is outside of you, separate from you, not part of you.

In your question, however, you create polarity. Are we here or are we there? And if we're there, where? Which dimension? But as you reemerge back into the Isness of All That Is, which is possible for every single one of you, as you elevate your own consciousness into your natural state of pure love, you will come into an understanding of your true oneness with all things. You will come into unity, into God consciousness, and you will stop seeing yourselves as being separate from anything, including us. And you will see that you were never separate from any of your other beloved teachers. It is all one.

We are simply in higher, formless dimensions of consciousness and therefore in a higher frequency that cannot be seen with your limited human senses. There are many dimensions, and later we'll speak more about this. What's important for you to know right now is that we are not separate from anything. We are not here and not there, and neither are you.

Your vibration and your level of consciousness determine what dimension you experience in any moment.

Those in a lower vibration, for example, simply do not yet perceive the pure love, the oneness, the unity, the God consciousness that they always are—still, they are not separate from us. And never is there a hierarchy; one is not better than any other.

Since you just mentioned that we can practice raising our levels of consciousness, which is what Sara tells us is necessary to channel, can you please explain channeling?

Channeling is the word you use to describe the very natural process of tuning in to the infinite intelligence that is always available to you in every moment. While everyone has access to this level of wisdom, awareness, consciousness, and perspective, very few ever tune in in a way that allows them to realize their own connection to Source, or with enough frequency for it to be as satisfying and gratifying to your physical senses as hearing these words through Sara to you.

Channeling is very natural. When an athlete is in "the zone," they have opened to Source energy; they're allowing greater access to the intelligence within them that is always available to them. When a musician sits down and plays a beautiful piece of inspired music that just flows through them, this is a form of channeling. When an artist sits down to paint a masterpiece and Source energy flows through them and their brush to the canvas, this is also a form of channeling. When you are sitting with a friend having a beautiful, loving conversation and suddenly your words flow through you, and you don't remember what you said, but you can remember the feeling of love, the chills you felt in the truth that flowed through you, this is channeling.

Every single one of you can tune in to Source—either through automatic writing or doing things that bring you joy and that allow you to play and create in ways that are fun for you. Many will consciously choose to tune in in ways that connect them to their guides, their angels, their councils, and similar collectives that are always available to them. None of this is ever separate from any one of you; it's simply of your choosing.

Very few channel intentionally because of the level of focus it takes to raise your vibration to the place where you can meet this level of consciousness to fully open and allow it to flow through you. We assure you, however, that all of you have unintentionally and spontaneously channeled in some way in your life. We also assure you that you can learn how to consciously and intentionally tune in to this infinite intelligence and channel for yourself and others.

In this instance, the wisdom that Sara is bringing forth is coming to her from you, The Council, which you have defined as a collective of our higher selves, as opposed to, perhaps, an individual's higher self, in the example of an athlete or artist. To be more specific, when Beethoven was composing his music, was there an intermediary like The Council, or was it his higher self only? Was Jesus speaking from the highest version of himself or from a collective?

It's all Source energy. There's no need to delineate it, or separate it, or give it a special name. You are all extensions of that which some of you call God and yet you all express as personalities. It is your intention of what you wish to bring forth that summons its source.

As you focus into this dimension of consciousness, where you have experiences of individuals and personalities and groups and collectives and families and all sorts of things, there is an adaptiveness to the way that you experience the energy you summon.

It is correct to say that collectives express differently through the channel or conduit through which they channel. Some of it is the personality of the higher collective, and some of it is the personality of the higher self of the channel.

When you tune in to this vibration, it takes on its own expression beyond what most of you would recognize as a human's personality. It feels more expansive to you. Labeling it, however, takes you away from the vibration of it into the thinking mind. We understand that you are doing this to help your human understand and compartmentalize it, but in labeling it you are limiting its expression.

Although we understand why it's so important for your logical minds to be able to create names and associations to identify different energies, we remind you of what we said first to you: while our words to you are important, this is a vibrational experience. It is the vibration that causes the transformation.

**So, what is personality?
When it comes to humans, isn't it
all the same divine energy or God flowing
through unique vessels that we call "me" or
"you," adapted by a person's understanding
of themself and life, filtered by
their beliefs and ideas?**

Your physical senses are always interpreting your experience, and that's what you call reality. However, Source energy is at such a high frequency and vibration that it's difficult to perceive with your physical senses. As such, your natural tendency is to find some way of identifying this energy. One way of doing this is to create a unique personality for it. This is fun for you and allows your human to find a level of intimacy with the energy, consciousness, and wisdom such that you can then allow it in for your expansion. For the enjoyment of self-discovery and expression, you're here to experience uniqueness. You're here to experience preference. You're here to experience all of your many other chosen traits and characteristics as you express yourself in physical form. Thusly, you create your personality.

Your unique personalities are of your own creation. You have created your personalities as a way of expressing yourself in physical form as the God that you are, and it's perfect. And yet the more you raise your consciousness and vibration, the more you align to the Source energy within you, the more playful you will be, the more humorous you will be, the more lighthearted you will be, and the more intelligent you will be, because your intelligence isn't coming from a memorization in the brain, it's coming from infinite intelligence.

So, while there are some who express higher levels of consciousness in a way that is very calm and very peaceful, others may express higher levels of consciousness in a way that's very fun and playful. It's all perfect and of your choosing.

What about the initial spark for a person to exist? By extension, who are we and where did we come from?

You are a force field of consciousness that is not limited to physical form or to a physical body. It has served you in the past to understand you have a spirit or a soul, and that is correct. Some call it a higher self; it's all perfectly well and good. That's how your human can begin to perceive the part of you that's more than what you've been able to perceive with your physical senses.

You're now focused in a physical body, and because that's all you know within the 3rd Dimension of consciousness, it is difficult to imagine yourself as a force field of consciousness, much less identify yourself as Source, or light.

Yet, this is what you are. You are consciousness. You are Source. You are light. You are that which you call God. And from the perspective of being one with Source, as this force field of consciousness, made up of particles of infinite creation that are always responding to you and your soul, your adventure began when you focused upon this human experience, thereby summoning the particles of infinite creation, which created your birth into physical form at this precise time.

Throughout every stage of your development, you drew to you from your environment everything you needed. Before your birth it was the womb of your mother from which you drew to you everything you needed to grow a physical body. There was an intelligence, a consciousness, that allowed you to expand, thrive, and develop into the manifestation that you call a baby.

You came from and still are pure Source energy. You came from and still are pure consciousness. You came from and still are pure light. You came from and still are pure love. And while it may seem that you were a helpless baby, your intelligence and consciousness drew to you everything that you needed to grow and develop into a toddler, into a young child, into a young adult, and into an adult. And your intelligence and consciousness make up the force field responsible for the continuous regeneration and rejuvenation of your cells, day in and day out.

What most of you would call God, Source, the Divine, Creator—it is all infinite Source energy. Through an unquantifiable number of years, you have continuously focused the Source energy that is you and evolved it into all sorts of different forms. Everything is Source energy.

Some suggest that the creative act of splitting off from Source and focusing yourself into different experiences throughout the universe is some sort of de-evolution—that you are somehow fallen angels in this Earthly experience and have great lessons to learn or terrible karma to correct. Yet nothing could be further from the truth. You are here in this human experience, absolutely and unequivocally, of your own choosing, because this is the best thing going on anywhere. *You have chosen to be here on Earth during the greatest transformation of human consciousness that has ever occurred in any lifetime.*

You, as this force field of consciousness, came from Source, and you will return to Source, because Source is what you are. And how magnificent is it that you are on this grand adventure?

You can imagine your multidimensionality like this: you are a person with a wonderful life. You have a beautiful home, a wonderful family, and work that you love. You really enjoy your life. Then one day, your curiosity is piqued about something—let's say it's another beautiful place in this world—maybe through inspiration, research, or simply because someone tells you about this place. You begin to focus your force field of consciousness into this other beautiful place on the planet. It could be a culture you want to experience, something you want to see there, or people you want to meet.

You begin to focus your consciousness into another experience; meanwhile you are still in physical form wherever you happen to be here on Earth. Yet now there is another part of you traveling across the world, so to speak, to this place you desire to explore. It is independent of you, yet part of you. And both, quite possibly, are unaware of the other. Together, however, both aspects of you are still of the same force field of consciousness. You are multidimensional; you can project your consciousness into different experiences. And as you have new experiences, you're relating data and information that leads to even greater expansion and more potentials and possibilities.

You're still Source energy. You're still God. You're still the Divine. You're still light. Whether you're focusing this force field on your day-to-day life or on an adventure you wish to have in another place and time.

THE COUNCIL'S DIMENSION AND REALITY

Are you more than what you bring to us? Do you have your own existence, your own lives, your own pursuits, your own adventures, your own hopes, your own dreams that are beyond our comprehension?

From our level of consciousness, *we are the dream*. We are realized in a vibration where all potentials and possibilities exist simultaneously. At this level of consciousness, there is no delay in manifestation. Desire and manifestation are one in the same. Yet there remain infinite potentials for further creation in every moment. You, on the other hand, are in an experience of time and space. You are in a level of density, in a dimension of consciousness where you are creating in physical form as you experience yourself in physical form.

We are not limited to physical form; we can perceive through you and experience physical form through you, but we are formless. We are nonphysical. And so there's no delay, lack, limitation, or separation from our experience ever. The dream, meaning anything that we can imagine in the moment, is our experience. There is no wanting, no waiting.

If you think about archangels, ascended masters, God, Jesus, or those who are in "Heaven," you don't think about lack. You also don't think about limitation, fear, struggle, or suffering. These don't exist in higher levels of consciousness, and there's a part of you that understands this. In higher dimensions there is only peace, joy, harmony, abundance, well-being, and freedom. But in lower dimensions you may create experiences of lack, limitation, fear, struggle, and suffering.

As you *intentionally* move into higher levels of consciousness and become aware that you can focus yourself into any experience that you wish, while continuing to be in physical form, you will be creating as we create. You will be creating as the master that you are.

How will your human experience these higher levels of creation? More peace, more joy, more harmony, more abundance, more well-being, and more freedom. And you become increasingly aware of new potentials for yourself, humanity, and Earth. You go beyond lack and wanting; everything you need shows up even before you know you need it. You live in such a flow, letting energy and light guide the way, that it just comes to you. This is ultimate alignment with True Creation, or impeccable creation, which we define as creation with no personal agenda. In

True Creation people, places, and circumstances that support your highest expression always arrive on time, and it's a "Yes!"

In your reality, is there continued expansion? Is there ambition? Is there an adventure underway all the time? These may be terms that only apply to us in the density of time, space, and matter, but are there any parallels?

Your expansion contributes to our expansion, and our expansion contributes to yours. In this, there is an expansion of the universe that all of us, in every dimension of consciousness, are contributing to, are part of, and are receiving benefit from.

We are always in our magnificence, our brilliance, our enthusiasm, our excitement. We are always in a state of inspiration because we are not creating stories and beliefs of lack or perceiving ourselves as limited, unworthy, or not good enough.

Do you have direction and intention unrelated to us? Again, are you more than who we have summoned?

Indeed, we have both our own direction and intention. Beyond what you might now imagine. Yet still, integral to our direction and intention is living in your physical form, as you. Living your life. Your lives and how they fit into the larger scheme of creation are what we want to help you understand.

You've created a belief that you began living when you were born and that you will stop living when you die; you call that your life. And what you create each day is what you call living. We're beyond this experience. There are no beginnings or endings; all is eternal. And yet, as we said, you are us and we are you. So we understand your experience, and when you are in higher levels of consciousness, you will have a better understanding of ours. Think of us as the expanded version of you—the part of you that exists beyond time and space.

You are in a dimension of consciousness, because of the rate of vibration you're in, where you experience time and space; you experience the illusion of birth and death. We just are. There's living, which is what you perceive yourself to be doing, and then what you might call a state of being, which is our experience. We are the Isness of All That Is, and that is what you are as well.

We don't have days like you have, but we understand that you're experiencing time this way. It's fun to experience time through days, weeks, months, and years. That's part of your journey. Our highest words to you, as you are experiencing this thing you call life, are to *live it to the fullest.* Live fully, love fully, and be all that you are in every moment. This is a choice—to either allow all that you are, or doubt and deny it through your stories of lack, limitation, and separation.

There's a whole lot more going on here than you can see or perceive with your limited human perspective or senses. But much of it would just be a distraction for you. Your chosen part in this game is to be in physical form. You focused yourself into physical form to be on the planet at this time and to learn how to access higher levels of consciousness and awareness to enrich the life you know. As you do this, your elevated vibration and consciousness leads to the elevation of humanity's vibration and consciousness.

What's most important is you coming fully into the realization of all that you are and living as the embodied master that you are. As we said, live fully, love fully, be all that you are, and create your reality the way you want it to be.

When you release the density of the body and continue your journey into higher levels of consciousness, within formless realities, you will continue to create and expand. You will be beyond the illusion of separation, and you will return to infinite peace, bliss, and love—the knowing of which is also available to you now.

The primary reason we come forth is to expand your awareness, to offer you a grander perspective, and to bring you into higher levels of vibration and consciousness so that you can remember the truth within you. This awareness can be yours now, and it will bring you into states of Heaven on Earth and higher levels of consciousness within this New Earth that will amaze, surprise, and delight you. It will also enable you to experience a life beyond your wildest dreams.

Your second question, about being more than what you have summoned, is very linear because you know yourself to be a singular being. While you have drawn this experience to you, we exist beyond it.

You believe you are the name and personality with which you identify. You believe that whatever you're doing on any given day, well, that's you and your experience. You're experiencing yourself and your reality through your physical senses—what you see, hear, taste, touch, and smell—and that's what you are calling your reality. It's your physical senses interpreting for you what's going on or what you're doing or what you're focused upon.

We don't live in that level of consciousness. We are one with all of creation at all times. For us, there is no doing. We are always in a dance with all of creation.

And is there more? Oh, there's always more. There's always more.

Again, there are many levels of consciousness beyond ours; some are at such high rates of vibration and frequency they go beyond the light; they are the Source of the light itself. Is it known from our level of consciousness that this potential exists and is a part of the path? Indeed. Are we perceiving from this level? We're only aware of it; however, we're not perceiving from it because of the state of consciousness in which we are focused.

There are different levels of consciousness. Most who are in the human experience are in the 3rd Dimension, which, as we said, is the dimension of separation. As you begin to raise your vibration and your consciousness, you will come into the 4th Dimension, which is the dimension of transformation, where you begin to understand that you can change your circumstances and conditions and heal from the past by elevating your thoughts—out of the past, out of the old, out of the struggle.

Many of you are now becoming aware of the 5th Dimension, which is the dimension of pure love. It's what you call Christ consciousness, unity consciousness, or oneness consciousness. The vibration of this dimension is what creates Heaven on Earth, or the New Earth. And you remembering this level of consciousness is what was meant by the Second Coming of the Christ; it is the experience of you coming into the state of Christ consciousness while remaining in physical form. This is upon you now! We, and many others, are here to emphasize the exciting potential you possess for achieving these realizations while remaining in physical form. In the past, most enlightened beings achieving such a state would simply ascend and leave the density of the body. Now, you need not choose this, as the path exists for you to self-realize and stay in human form, remaining as wayshowers for all of humanity, as you revel in the freedoms that are your birthright.

There are also the 6th, 7th, and 8th Dimensions, which are more formless realities. We reside in these realms, where we can still find a vibrational resonance to connect with you, especially when your vibration is high. Again, there are many dimensions of consciousness even beyond those. Are these energies sometimes part of the experience? Yes. However, they are at a very high vibration and frequency and are better understood from our perspective where we're not trying to understand it through the limitation of the human mind.

Do you feel incomplete because you're not at those higher levels yet? As a human, perhaps because of my angst or a fleeting sense of lack, I personally feel a hunger—almost to a point of displeasure. I want to be further along; I want to see more, to know more. Do you feel incomplete, or do you feel complete?

We are always in the truth and in the knowing of your wholeness, your completeness, your perfection; and we are always in the truth and knowing of ours. From our perspective, it is all perfect even while always expanding and becoming more. There are infinite potentials and possibilities. And we are always following the energy; there is no lack or limitation. Similarly, you can come into your wholeness and completeness and continue to create and expand from there. As you begin to step into even higher levels of consciousness where more and more is possible and available to you, you're not so attached to whether your desires manifest in form or formless. Ultimately, we see all your desires as a desire for more wholeness, oneness, fullness, completeness, and expansion.

And that fills you? I suppose if a human could come into feeling their wholeness and sense their completeness, they'd probably be less in a hurry to get beyond the human experience.

Indeed. If you're on a vacation and having a wonderful time, you know you're going to go home eventually. But you're having such a wonderful time. You enjoy your vacation. You enjoy your adventure. You know you're going to go home eventually. But right here, right now in this moment, this vacation is the best thing going on! And that's how we want you to view your human experience: as a grand vacation, a grand adventure of your making.

We know we came from Source and will return to Source. We know Source is what we are. And we know that in time we'll go beyond the light to become one with the Source of light again. In the meantime, we're having a magnificent adventure ourselves here and with all of you

How do things happen in your dimension? Do you simply allow things to happen, without "pushing" or "efforting"? Or do you create from personal or collective desires? Do you direct energy, or do you just surrender to Source energy?

We're always creating. We're always co-creating. We're just not in a dimension of consciousness where we believe in a lack of time or separation, so we are always in allowing, aligned to Source energy. As we said before, there is no wanting. Your desires come from believing that you're separate from that thing that you desire, when truly you are not. We do not experience desires as you do because we are not in an experience of separation.

There is your truth, and then there is expansion and creation from your truth. The truth of who you are is love, joy, peace, harmony, well-being, abundance, freedom, beauty, power. As you embody this truth, and then expand and create in alignment with it, you will be creating from a place of wholeness, like we are, rather than from lack.

Where or how does God, or call it Source energy, fit into this equation?

To even try to explain God, Source, Creator, the Infinite, the Divine so that the human mind can understand it, immediately limits it. While we can give you some brief answers here that will satisfy your brain and begin to expand your awareness, we invite you to feel for the power of God that is within you, that flows through you, that is you. We also invite you to begin to experience the God within others and within all things. There will come a moment of realization where you will know what God is because you can feel it from your state of being, and there will be no need for words. Our words here are beginning to tune your awareness so that you can open and allow your human to experience and know the part of you that is God.

God is the ultimate creator. It is the energy in all things, and it is the energy that creates all things. It is Source. We say that everything is made of particles of infinite creation, and these particles are always responding to you. Is there an intelligence behind it? Yes, consciousness, God consciousness. This is the intelligence, for example, that beats your heart, grows your hair, and regenerates the cells in your body. And as you continue to elevate your consciousness beyond the illusion of separation, you will feel this God consciousness within you and have greater access to its intelligence, enabling it to do so much more for you. More than you can even imagine.

We remind you that you are creator within your own creation. You are the center of your universe. As we said, you focused yourself into the 3rd Dimension of consciousness, into the density of physical form. You summoned the particles of infinite creation so that you could experience yourself in form, as separate and unique and as having a distinct personality. You have free will. So you choose experiences for yourself: you try new things, and you create yourself as an individual—all the while continuously summoning particles of infinite creation through your focus on the reality that you are creating for yourself.

Nothing went wrong here. This is a great privilege. This is an incredible experience. It is a grand adventure. And when you're ready to leave this Earth plane and continue your exploration into higher dimensions, you will release the density of the body and reemerge into the vibrational truth of who you are. In these levels of consciousness, you will know yourself as God.

Yet as you continue forward on this Earthly journey—through different levels of consciousness within the human experience—you will remember the God within you and within all others and in everything. You will remember yourself as the Isness of All That Is within all of creation. This is what we mean by realization. Then you will dance and play with all of creation as the self-realized master that you are.

In this level of consciousness, the 5th Dimension, you are not trying to fix anything or make anything happen, and you don't believe in lack, limitation, fear, or separation. Instead, you come fully into your power as the God that you are, creator within your own creation, remembering how fun it is to create your reality in any way you wish it to be. It all becomes so much easier and enjoyable.

And so you have come to us now to help us remember these things. You are our future selves, reaching back saying, "All is well, all is possible, you are powerful, life is beautiful." Is this it in a nutshell?

Indeed. We are beyond the illusion that you believe yourself to be. We're not better or more powerful than you; we simply have a grander perspective. Imagine that levels of consciousness are like steps leading up a staircase with many steps. Each step is a different level of consciousness, with different perspectives and different experiences and potentials. It's like climbing to the top of a mountain. As you get higher and higher, you have a far greater view, a greater perspective; you can see a bigger picture as you go higher up the mountain. As you allow yourself into higher levels of consciousness, you begin to see a much grander perspective of the human experience. It was understood at the start of your adventure on Earth that you would be focusing into an experience of separation; and you knew at just the perfect time you would awaken to this and come into the realization of all that you are—the grander perspective, so to speak, of you. And it is all perfect.

These higher levels of consciousness are not better. No one is better than another because they're in a higher level of consciousness. But oh, your life will be so much easier, so much more fun, and so much happier in higher levels of consciousness. It will also be much more abundant and full of peace, joy, love, harmony, well-being, and freedom.

We understand you've been in this human experience for so long that you really do believe yourselves to be what your physical senses are interpreting about you and your reality. And yet, we always see you as the truth of who you are, the master that you are.

You say that you came forth because you promised you would. Is it because we're open and asking? Have you agreed to meet us here at this particular time and place to bring us truths that we've been missing?

It wasn't even an agreement; it simply can be no other way. When you come into this level of consciousness, where we are now, you're expanding your perspective, you're elevating your level of consciousness, which opens whole new worlds to you. We've been here all along—even when you were in fear, when you were in grief, when you were struggling, when you were suffering. When you're at such a dense rate of vibration—and we do not mean this with any judgment or disrespect—there's a heaviness and a slowing of your vibration. In these states, you are so far from the truth of you and from where we are. Using our previous analogy, you are at the bottom of the staircase, and we are at the top. When you were in these states, there were many steps separating us on the staircase. You could not hear or even sense us, nor could you feel the vibrational truth of who you really were. But we were always there, always with you.

This is still the reason why so many people feel alone and isolated, often suffering from the densest human emotions, shame and grief.

Shame is the heaviest human emotion—when you are telling yourself stories about something terrible that happened when you were a child, or some mistake you made, or something that you did to someone or that they did to you. When you are holding on to such fears, you are as far as you can be from the truth of you.

Many of you spend a lot of time grieving, simply because you're in the human experience. You have been influenced by others and their beliefs, including religious and societal beliefs. You may believe you're a sinner, that you're here to correct some horrible karmic debt, or that you're some sort of fallen angel, here to suffer, or to be punished, or to right your wrongs, your family's wrongs, or humanity's wrongs . . . .

Because of these influences, you think that you're here to fix yourself and a broken world. You think you are here to carry these burdens on your shoulders. You believe you're not enough—not good enough. You don't realize how much you are grieving. Meanwhile, these feelings, these choices, continue to entangle you in an experience of separation.

When you remember the truth of who you are, why you are here, and all that you intended; when you remember how magnificent you are and how magnificent your life is meant to be; when you remember that you are the creator within your own creation of reality, that there is a grander perspective, and that there is a higher level of consciousness always available to you; you set yourself free. In the moment that you remember, you come into realization, and the past is healed. You feel whole and complete again, although you always were.

Separation is an illusion. Unworthiness is an illusion. Grief is an illusion. Shame is an illusion. Fear is an illusion. It's all coming from a story you're telling yourself—from the thoughts that you are thinking. You can tell how closely aligned your thoughts are to the truth of who you are by the way you feel.

The thoughts you think affect your emotions. Your emotions affect the way that you feel. The way that you feel affects the vibration and the level of consciousness you are able to experience, which determines the reality that you are creating. It really is this simple; it all comes from the thoughts you have.

You, our dear friend, know so very well that *thoughts become things*. This is the foundation of your teachings. You also know that you can change your thoughts. You can change your stories. But do this from a place of being rather than thinking. The power of your consciousness and awareness is what allows for this. When you drop from your head to your heart, you begin to sense that you are more than your thoughts, more than your stories. You begin to sense the God consciousness that you truly are. In this level of consciousness, you begin to see the greater truth of who you are and what is going on here; this alone will elevate you out of the shame and the grief. Then, as you spend more time in this level of consciousness, you will begin to feel the freedom, the abundance, the love, the joy, and the harmony that is you, and that has always been here for you.

We simply cannot go into suffering with you; it's too far from our vibration—yet we love you so much. We can explain suffering and why it happens on your planet. And, as we said, you feel so awful in these lower states of consciousness, in the heavier, denser emotions, because of the thoughts that you're thinking—which are due to the mistruths you're telling yourself, about others, and about what's going on in your lives or the world. This is why you feel so hopeless and isolated in these states. Suffering—like unworthiness, separation, grief, shame, and fear—is also an illusion. Some say life is about suffering. Some even think that their purpose for being here is to suffer. And we tell you this couldn't be further from the truth.

Yet there is no judgment from our side ever. It is understood that these and other illusions exist in lower dimensions. We also know—whether now or in the moment you make your transition—that you will come back into the truth of who you are and see all of this from a grander perspective, fully aligned with your truth and the knowing within you.

You work really hard to believe in your unworthiness, and you get stuck in lower vibrations because you believe in it. However, it takes a lot of energy to maintain these lower vibrational states because they are not the truth of you. Think of it as if you are trying to hold a soccer ball under water; the ball just wants to rise to the surface. Let it. Let your true nature rise to the surface. It's as simple as closing your eyes and taking three deep breaths; this will bring you back into the moment. Then put your attention in your heart area and begin to feel for the awareness of the truth of you; see if you can sense the spaciousness, the expansiveness. In a matter of seconds, you can be in a higher state of consciousness.

ANGELS AND HELPERS

How might you compare yourself to angels? You mentioned them earlier, along with guides. Are you angels to us or is that another realm of helpers? And what about archangels?

There are many realms of consciousness around you all the time. There are elemental realms, fairy realms, archangel realms, angel realms, ascended master realms, and others. There are all sorts of realms, each with unique vibrational signatures. They are all extensions of Source, just like you are an extension of Source. They focus in different levels of consciousness with different and unique experiences within those levels of consciousness. Some of you may feel a deep connection to certain realms, like that of the angels, which is perfect for those who choose such. We, however, identify most closely with the ascended master realms of consciousness.

I have understood that angels exist exclusively for us, as if their entire focus and mission and existence is being a lifeline for those in time and space. Is that true?

Indeed. But again, it is from their highest choosing, as their highest form of expression, because that's the adventure they most wanted to have.

Whereas you are us but in higher levels of consciousness, and on other adventures, simultaneously reaching back to give us a hand in our evolution. Is that fair? I'm still trying to understand who you are!

Our particular focus, in this expression you are experiencing, is guiding you to live your highest potential within the human experience as the ascended masters that you are. Much of what we focus upon and the wisdom we bring forth is related to this. Here we are focused on co-creating with you by way of these exchanges. This is also part of Sara's highest joy and excitement. Because of her deep interest in guiding others and her focus into the level of consciousness in which we exist, together we bring forth this co-created vibrational experience that you call the channeling or the wisdom of The Council.

If someone had an experience as a child where they were scared, for example, and then felt or saw the presence of an angel that comforted them, it's likely that they're going to continue to stay open to the angelic realm. They may find great interest in that realm.

There is familiarity. There is resonance. There is alignment. They may be drawn to read books on angels. They may seek to connect to angels. They may also become a conduit by which angels communicate through them. Maybe even an aspect of themselves—a higher dimensional aspect—will focus itself into a vibrational reality of serving as if they were an angel to others on Earth. Some may choose archangels, and yet others may choose to connect with collectives of different beings, such as Pleiadeans and Arcturians. There are all sorts of unique expressions of consciousness available to you in different realities throughout the universe.

Everything is an aspect of you, an extension of you. Again, you are a multidimensional being. You can focus yourself into any reality you choose. If someone says to us, "I heard the name Pleiadean, and I really gravitated toward that," it means there is some familiarity, some interest, or some experience of theirs that is remembering this connection. They might then begin to focus their consciousness to align to the vibration where the Pleiadean consciousness exists and move that vibration and consciousness into an experience of physical form.

We know it's incredibly difficult for your human to understand that the Pleiadeans, the Arcturians, the ascended masters, and the archangels are all extensions of you—just as we are. However, as you move beyond time and space, limitation, separation, and the experiences of being in physical form on Earth, you will realize there is no separation. Communication is completely transparent; everything is known. There is a recognition of different vibrational frequencies, vibrational imprints, and signatures of various uniqueness, if you wish to call it that, but it does not mean you are separate from anything.

LIVING YOUR PURPOSE

You've said this book of ours (yours, mine, and Sara's) is a co-creation . . .

Did your summoning and asking draw this to you? Absolutely. Did Sara's focus upon seeking and drawing these answers to her questions create this experience of channeling answers through her? Absolutely. Anyone who is receiving this message, whenever it might be, is also channeling this wisdom to themselves.

You expanded your consciousness through your asking and in that moment the answer was there. The best part of it from our perspective is that you think you came up with the question, but most every question you ask is an inspiration that came through you from your higher self for the expansion of your consciousness here on Earth and beyond.

Remember, you are creator within your own creation of your reality. You are a force field of consciousness made up of particles of infinite creation. You can limit this force field of consciousness to think you are just this body, or you can expand this force field of consciousness to know that you are the universe, that you are God, that you are creator, and then begin to perceive yourself into all that you are.

There is a greater dream, a greater vision, a greater purpose for you being on the planet at this time. Some of you have felt this greater calling within you. You wouldn't be having this experience if there weren't some aspect of you that knows there is a purpose for you being here. You may not consciously know what that is—yet—but there is another part of you that does know.

You matter, and it is important that you're here. In the chapters to come, we will answer your questions about the dream, the journey, eternity, and God, which will bring you into far greater awareness of who you are and why you are here. It will provide you with a much grander perspective of what you intended when you chose to focus yourself into this very human experience.

Remember that you are perceiving through your senses—what you see, what you hear, what you taste, what you touch, what you smell, and what you think. As you expand your awareness and consciousness, you will begin to perceive beyond your senses. You will come into knowing, which is a greater feeling state, connected to the state of being. And you will understand the difference of creating from that place and that level of alignment to Source.

You are here with a purpose. You *are* your purpose. Being on the planet at this specific time, awakening to truth and coming into realization is your purpose. And your unique journey—the path you took, and the trails you blazed—they're important, they matter, and they are also your purpose.

You cannot get this wrong. You are contributing to the elevation of consciousness on the planet. You are contributing to raising the vibration on the planet. You are seeding human consciousness with infinite potentials and possibilities, just by living fully, loving fully, and being all that you are. Creating your reality the way you wish it to be is the most important thing you can do, because as you come into the realization of the joy, the love, the peace, the harmony, the freedom, the well-being, and the abundance that is you and is here for you, you are seeding human consciousness with this potential for all who are also ready to remember.

Again, you didn't come here to fix a broken world or to drag everyone over the finish line to the Promised Land. To every reader of these words: *you are wayshowers.* You are here to show humanity the way into higher levels of consciousness.

Because you are in an experience of free will, you have the freedom to choose the thoughts that you are thinking, the stories that you are telling, and the level of consciousness in which you are focused. You have the freedom to choose any experience you wish to create, moment by moment. And as you do, you will serve in ways unimaginable.

This magnificent adventure is just beginning. Allow yourself to realize the truth of who you are. Allow yourself to live the magnificent life that you intended when you chose to focus yourself into this human experience. Allow this to be a grand adventure!

SECTION 2

THE DREAM

In this section, The Council explores the very reason for life as we know it.

Greetings, Council, it's such a privilege to be with you and Sara and to talk about the dream—the dream of life. The first question I have for you is, what was God's or Source energy's dream for life in time and space? What was the origin, what was the impetus, what was the desire, what was the hope for this big splash into the illusions of time, space, and matter?

Now, there is a grand plan here; there is a master plan. If we could summarize it for you, we would say the plan is for expansion. While Source is always whole and complete, it is always expanding into more. Your part of the plan is to be in the experience of form, or density. As you begin to expand into new levels of creation and consciousness within your human experience, new levels of potential and possibility become available to you and your human family.

Ultimately, you will return to Source, while forever retaining your own integrity. You will not dissolve or disappear! You will return to the Divine with a knowing that all the data and information you collected here—all the ways you explored and expressed yourself, and all the experiences that you had—led to your expansion and to the expansion of the entire universe and Source itself.

Are my dreams for myself the same as God's or Source's dream for me?

God's or Source energy's dream for you is the same as your soul's dream for you—realization—to know yourself as that which you call God. And to know that you are not separate from God even though you're in a 3-Dimensional experience, which is the dimension of separation. However, as we've said, the 3rd Dimension is a dimension of free will, which means that you can choose what you'd like to experience while in form: you can create from and experience the separation from lower levels of self-awareness, where there may be great suffering, or you can create from and experience higher levels of consciousness, where there is only love, joy, peace, freedom, abundance, and well-being.

We would say, therefore, that the greatest dream for you, and your greatest opportunity here, is to fully embody the Source energy, God consciousness. In this, you will experience more fun, more magic, and more miracles. It is the state of consciousness where grand and glorious manifestations come to you out of the blue, and people, ideas, and inspirations show up that can take your life to another level. From there, your experience just continues to expand, getting better and better. Such a realization of Self is where it's at because it puts you in touch with all that you are, including higher levels of intelligence that are available in higher dimensions of consciousness.

Self-realization, or realization, is to come fully into the understanding of who you are—the God, the light, the pure Source energy that you are.

As you come into realization, you will begin to know the power within you; seeing yourself as pure potential and possibility for whatever you can imagine. Then you will understand that what you are truly wanting, beneath all your surface desires, is to realize more of the pure Source energy, God consciousness that is you. And as you fully allow this to be realized, you discover the power you've had all along to be the most magnificent creator within your own Heaven on Earth.

You came from God. You came from Source. But in the meantime, you are here on a grand adventure. It's fun to express yourself as an aspect of the Divine. It's fun to create yourself uniquely. It's fun to create your reality the way you wish it to be, and your experience on Earth only gets better as you remember the God that you are. This human experience is like no other in all the universe; here you are in a dimension where you get to choose what happens next.

Without realization, however, you create unintentionally. Unknowingly, you sometimes choose the unwanted. You call these realities the nightmares, the terrors, the mistakes, and the experiences of struggle and suffering. Yet the dream of Heaven on Earth is always within you. You may think of Heaven as a fairytale, or a Promised Land—reserved for an experience beyond time and space—but we assure you the dream of Heaven on Earth is just as available to anyone and everyone who is choosing it here as it is a reality in higher dimensions. Yet you have forgotten that you can choose. We come forth to remind you of this dream within your heart, which you never intended to forget.

THE MYSTERY OF TIME

I recognize that there's no destiny because of free will. But how do we reconcile that everything is happening in "the now," all at once? And what about the things we don't perceive?

When you are one with Source and the Divine, everything is now, everything is known, everything is here; there is no lack of anything. You focused yourself into the human experience to be part of all that exists here, which is the experience of linear time.

You knew at some point you would wake up and remember that time is simply a collective human creation—an agreed-upon manifestation. In this realization, you'll understand that time isn't linear; it's more circular or spherical in nature. Combining this truth with an understanding that everything is infinite, you can begin to tune in to all the different timelines of potential and possibility that are available to you in any moment.

Because you are in the experience of physical form, with free will, you get to choose which timelines you explore and experience. This is how you start using time as a tool that works for you.

In each moment you are choosing from all the potentials and possibilities that exist in your awareness at that time. All are expressions of you, and all will lead to your expansion. Within the human experience there are multiple different timelines and yet everything is happening now. You may choose a particular timeline or path to follow, but there is never, at any time, a wrong path and a right path. Every path will lead you back to you. You are always going to find your way home.

You said we can learn how to use time. What comes to mind is that with free will, there exists likelihoods and probabilities of future events. Do you mean by "using time" we can choose probabilities based on what we envision?

You often think of things as up there or out there. You focus on the stars, and you think that the universe is up there, out there, when everything is actually within you. While it might be difficult for your human to believe, you really are the center of your universe: all the dimensions of consciousness available to you are within you, and every timeline is too. It's not up there or out there. But you think this way because you only believe yourself to be this physical body. When you think of your body, you think of what's inside—the bones, the muscles, a heart, two lungs, a brain. You think, "That's what's inside."

What we're referring to, including your likelihoods and probabilities, is also within you, but it's formless; it's your force field of consciousness. And if you were to feel into that, you would know it as multidimensional.

You come into this human experience as pure Source energy. Over time you become part of the human collective and are told what is possible for you. You are influenced by others' experiences and perceptions. If they believe they are limited by time, space, and geography, you will most likely believe that too.

You're creating your own reality of limitation through your beliefs; so, in essence, you're beholden to time. Instead, you could consciously move yourself into a dimension of awareness where time is working for you. In this level of consciousness, all kinds of potentials and possibilities become available to you—for example, traffic suddenly becomes lighter, you discover a new road to take, your client calls and says they're running late, and time expands.

I see. What do I do to *not* be beholden to time?

Perceive beyond the limitations of time that you've learned; this is the way to begin allowing time to serve you. You have a wonderful metaphor in the human experience related to the illusion of time; it is the story of the four-minute mile. First, it was believed that the mile could only be run in eight minutes. Later, for decades, runners attempted to break a four-minute mile and couldn't, so it was thought to be impossible. Then when it was done, something shifted in the collective consciousness. Now, more than a thousand people have broken that barrier. So, why can't humans run a one-minute mile?

The answer is because you cannot perceive it at this moment. Most people on the planet could not conceive of running a mile in eight minutes, let alone four. For those who can see themselves running an eight-minute mile, some might think, because it's happened, they could run a four-minute mile. But nearly all would doubt their ability to run a one-minute mile. And yet if you focused yourself into a dimension of consciousness where you are not limited to the experiences of time, space, and geography, you could absolutely run a one-minute mile.

The collective human consciousness has tremendous influence on what you believe is possible. For example, if you are headed to a destination that is supposed to take five hours, you could focus yourself into a dimension of consciousness where it takes less time. But if you have a bunch of people in the car with you who are perceiving the limitation of time, it's going to be very difficult for you to perceive yourself into another dimension of consciousness.

It is about moving yourself into an awareness and perspective beyond lack and limitation into greater potentials and possibilities. But don't do this from a lower level of consciousness, from a place of lack. In other words, don't try to manifest something to avoid an unwanted experience. For example, if you are really upset that you're going to be late, you might try to figure out how to make it to your destination so you're not late. Because you're stressed out and worried about the consequences of being late, you might try to force time to collapse, and circumstances to change, for you to be on time.

Let go of your ideas of what should be happening and of trying to force an outcome; know that you are exactly where you're meant to be, in perfect flow, in perfect harmony. Go into an awareness, a dimension of consciousness, where you perceive yourself beyond the limitation of time and space. This is a place of absolute flow and ease, a state of consciousness where you know, beyond a doubt, that you are reaching your destination at the perfect time.

If you focused totally on the state of joy and peace and ease that is available in this higher dimension of consciousness, you would likely arrive to your destination in less time, because you are perceiving yourself beyond the limitation of the "miles per hour" form of travel. And even if you are late, you would be having the experience of arriving at the perfect time, which can positively affect others' perceptions of it. But, again, that is not why you are doing it. You are doing it because there is so much more freedom and joy and ease and peace in these higher dimensions, which is your dream for this grand adventure.

This is an example of how you can allow time to serve you, but it's also an example of how you can use the power of your consciousness to create more of what you want and intended in this life experience. The first step is to become aware of the level of consciousness from which you are perceiving something. Are you perceiving it from the limited human perspective or from the grander perspective?

Does that mean we can bend time and circumstances to suit our higher vision, beyond the constraints of what society wants us to think or believe?

Perceive yourself into a level of awareness where you go beyond the previous believed constraints; this is most important. You are not trying to manipulate things in lower dimensions of consciousness, and you are not trying to force energy where you think it should go. Instead, by fully perceiving yourself into the Source energy or God consciousness that you are, you will be allowing that elevated energy to be used in the best way by Source.

We'll give you a perfect example of allowing. Would you agree that we, The Council, as well as what you call archangels, angels, and even extraterrestrials, are beyond the limitations of time and space? Can you imagine that we travel through the universe at a much greater velocity than what is available in the human experience?

The only difference between us and humans is the amount of Source energy being allowed. When you fully allow Source energy, you go beyond time and space, separation, and illusion.

You could even move your body into other geographical locations, instantly, by fully coming into alignment with Source energy, the God force, or the Christ consciousness and perceiving yourself into these experiences.

Now, the reason people don't do this every day, all day long is they aren't aware of such possibilities and the potentials. They haven't allowed themselves to perceive beyond their presently believed-in limits.

When you begin to understand that you are the creator of your reality, you will also understand that you can only create realities that you can imagine and believe as possible. As you continue to expand your awareness and perspective, you continue to expand the possibilities of what you can create within your experience.

The expansion starts by perceiving something new for yourself; through your awareness you can then allow your consciousness into it. By consciously perceiving what it is you'd like to be experiencing more of, you summon the particles of infinite creation that begin to draw to you everything you need to create that experience. *Consciousness is what moves energy into form; it is the formula for all creation.*

Your human is not going to figure out how to bend time. What it can do is learn how to open and allow Source energy—the God-force within you—to move you into dimensions of consciousness where you're perceiving beyond time to enable the Infinite to flow into your experience. That's when the magic and miracles occur.

When you notice yourself being beholden to time, rushing and hurrying, distracted by deadlines, lists, and other things that "have to be" done, catch yourself. Consciously and intentionally choose to become aware that there's another perspective available to you—a perspective where everything is exactly how it's supposed to be, in perfect flow, in perfect harmony.

Allow yourself into the awareness of this perspective and say to yourself, "Okay, I don't have to figure out how this is going to work. I don't have to force or effort here. I'm just going to elevate myself into a place of joy, freedom, feeling good, being at peace, going with the flow, and letting the energy and the light guide the way." Don't worry about how long it's going to take to get there. And don't just think it, feel it. Let the ease and effortlessness of this higher perspective flow through you. This is how to become the powerful creator of your own creation.

HUMANITY AND OUR FORGOTTEN ADVENTURE

How much of reality is composed of time and space–the physical universe–versus nonphysical? Are we just a drop in the ocean, or a much greater part than the nonphysical? How much of God's energy or focus is in this dimension versus elsewhere?

We understand the nature of your question, but you are asking the question because your human mind cannot perceive that you are God, and that's really all there is. You are still thinking that God is out there creating you and creating this or that, when it is more accurate to say that you are God. You are doing the creating. You are the center of your universe.

Again, the formula for creation is *consciousness moves energy into form*. Everything is energy. All energy has a nonphysical component, and most energy has a physical component. What you think of as "physical" is just lower-vibration energy. But it is your consciousness that moves this energy into form. How much of God's attention is on creation in physical form? The answer is 100 percent of it—because you are pure God, creating in physical form.

We'd like you to understand that for most of your life, your human—your magnificent human—has believed it is only human. We come forth to provide you with a greater awareness and understanding of all that you are. This is our primary objective. Questions about percentages, how much, and how big, that interest the human mind are far less important than your realization. Experiencing the truth of you is of primary importance. In your questions you're trying to drag the human into some other experience of the universe instead of allowing your human the entire experience of Self, which is within you, to be realized by you.

You are a multidimensional being—a part of you is focused on this human experience, while other parts of you are focused on other experiences in other dimensions. And as you begin to perceive and become more aware of these other-dimensional aspects of you, you will begin to integrate them into your experience. This is what we call realization. Realization is the remembering and integration of every part of you. It's not up there or out there. It is within this force field of consciousness that is you. In this sense, we are all within you—the angels, archangels, the ascended masters, Christ, God. It is all you.

Incredible. Thank you. Please further explain the concept of our supposed fall from grace.

The fall from grace? Grace, this feeling of pure bliss, one with Source, all-knowingness? Again, you think that it's up there, out there, and that you fell to Earth. This is another question from an experience of linear time.

From our perspective, you're here absolutely by your own choosing. You're in this magnificent adventure, this incredible human experiment, to fully experience all within it. But you're also here because the experiment is so fantastic.

And there's no shortage of time for humanity to come into realization and begin living at higher levels of consciousness to maximize this experience. It's not a time frame that you can get wrong, although there are opportunities where the energies are more supportive of your transformation, and now is one of these times. Your realization could even happen in an instant.

We'll give you another perspective on it. In the moment that you take your final breath and release the density of the body, you will reemerge back into nonphysical and come into higher levels of consciousness—into pure bliss, pure love, all-knowingness. From there, you will say, "Oh, I can't believe I made it that hard." You'll say, "Wait, let me go back. I remember now. I'm going to play. I'm going to have fun. I am creator within my creation, and everything was there for me: infinite resources, infinite abundance, infinite well-being, infinite love, and infinite intelligence were there the entire time. I just forgot." And you'll say, "Wait, let me go back now that I remember how much easier it was meant to be." But here is what we want you to know: you don't have to wait to release the density of the body to remember!

Was the forgetting intentional or was it an accident?

It was understood; it's part of the anticipated experience in this dimension.

The best way we can explain the human experience to you is through the metaphor of a movie. You watch movies and experience emotions from them. Yet you walk out of the movie theater knowing that you had an experience but that you were not actually that experience. Movies—like the experience of being in a human body—simply expand your experience within consciousness, which we define as having awareness or knowledge of something. There are so many things within your human experience that are reflecting to you why you would focus yourself into a particular experience and how it allows you into greater levels of self-expression.

Forgetting, then, is part and parcel of allowing ourselves to be swept away by the magic, love, and beauty that's all around us. We anticipated that we would forget; it was part of the plan. And no matter how much we've been stubbing our toes and crying, we are now, with your wisdom and the energies at hand, coming together to remember. Your assistance is part of this. We can awaken within the dreams of our lives and become the director of our movies, using free will to choose more wisely and begin to have more fun.

Indeed. Living fully awake within the dream is an opportunity. Exactly as you might awaken in a nighttime sleep-induced dream and realize you are dreaming. The irony, here, is that your nighttime dreams are closer to "true reality" than your waking dream of life.

There is some part of your consciousness that understands experience beyond the limitation of time, space, and place. You even have dreams while you're "sleeping," for example, where a loved one who has made their transition from physical to nonphysical is now there with you, expressing in physical form. In that state, you wouldn't say they were "gone." Which one is reality? Is the experience you have with them a dream, or is it reality? What you call your "awake" time, moving through your day, doing what you need to do, is more of the dream.

We are here to bring you into another level of awareness—a grander perspective of what's possible. You and our readers have created our meeting because you have begun to suspect that with more awareness, you can perceive yourself beyond limitation into infinite possibilities, which serves in the expansion of your soul, and which will add immeasurably to the joy of your human experience.

We love you magnificent humans! And if each of you would love your humans as we do and realize that your human gives you the opportunity to experience all that is here, more of you would fall in love with your human, and with the human experience. Your human being in form is allowing you to be part of this grand experiment, this grand adventure. Celebrate it! And begin to understand that what you really are is the awareness, the consciousness, that had created, and still creates, all that you perceive.

Now, for each one of us, why are we in the form we are? Who said, "We need a Mike Dooley, a Sara Landon, and a John Doe?" Or was it the evolution of consciousness that formed each of us? If so, can all souls project their consciousness into Earth? How do we understand our origins as individuals?

You came from Source. As consciousness, you focused yourself into physical form by first perceiving yourself as pure potential and possibility. Then you focused yourself into the force field of consciousness that is you. For a variety of different reasons, you chose a specific physical experience and all the details—where you were born, to whom you were born, and all else.

You're always choosing how you evolve and expand your consciousness, your soul, your spirit, your light, and the divine being that you are through the experiences you focus upon—through the initial circumstances of your life and the unfolding life experiences that you choose.

The elements of evolution are expansion, expression, and experiences. All these lead to the evolution of your soul and consciousness. Is there a higher purpose and reason, beyond what you can perceive, for your expansion, expression, and experiences; and does it lead to greater evolution? Absolutely.

Your human cannot even begin to understand how incredibly important your life experience is to the whole. And yet some would look at their life and say, "Well, I failed," or "I haven't done it right," or "Why would I ever choose to be me?" And yet, at any time in your life, by choosing to allow yourself to feel the Source energy that you are and know yourself as the center of your universe, you will realize that all those choices, all those experiences, led you to this moment of awareness. That's the perfection of it all.

UNDERSTANDING UNEXPECTED MANIFESTATIONS

How do we understand the unexpected that often just drops into our lives–the good, the bad, and the ugly that often seems random and unrelated to

anything we've knowingly been focusing on? Might such occurrences be examples of divine will?

There is only your will, which is as divine as there is. There is no true separation between you and Source energy. Such occurrences arise from your own deeper yearnings, understandings, and sometimes, your misunderstandings, yet all serve to awaken your power.

The "good," as you call it, always far outweighs the "bad and the ugly," yet it's the latter that likely prompts such questions, so we'll go there to help you understand.

Let's say, following your own reasons and rationale, you went to school, you went to college, or got a job, or joined the military. Either way, you launched yourself into the world, doing everything you thought you were supposed to do. Then one day, something happened that turned your life upside down. It could have been a diagnosis, an accident, a divorce, a violation, the death of a loved one, the collapse of a business or loss of a job or your home—anything that caused you to question life as you knew it.

In the face of such an event, you can't even imagine a silver lining. You're just in reaction and resistance. You don't want to lose what you have or what you think is you. Yet, in time, a direction emerges that you experience as better than anything you had ever known or felt before. Wisdom is imparted; you find your footing and emerge from the calamity as "more" than before it arose.

This may take some time, and of course, some will remain in denial, temporarily preventing their own advancement. But if you continued pressing on in your life, wasn't the "new you," who emerged from the circumstances emboldened, something you have also always wanted? Was it not a manifestation of your own inner desires for expansion and betterment? Weren't objectives achieved and progress made possible? Can you see that while the circumstances that made this possible may not have been desired, the outcome was? Do you still see this as divine will, or can you grasp that it was your own? That it was your earlier, innate ability to wonder and wish for your development, heightened confidence, improved stability, and control that found expression through navigating turmoil? Whether self-induced or part of a collective upheaval, as the manifestation of a collective desire for awakening and empowerment?

Many readers will be able to identify major upheaval and upleveling in their lives in the 2007–2009 time frame, and again between 2011 and 2013, and more recently from 2020 on. As you reflect on these time frames, you will recognize that things were not only happening in your life, but they were also happening in the lives of many others.

Know that your collective wills were alive and well at these times, guiding you to a fulfilment of your own greater desires. It's almost as if the energy is pulling you toward something, leading you toward some sort of anticipated illumination. We often say that Source knows the quickest, easiest, most effortless path between here and the dreams in your heart, but we are referring to the highest within you. The more you allow it, the more you are opening yourself up to receive the really big manifestations that come out of the blue through circumstances beyond your wildest dreams, to achieve shared objectives as well as those that are entirely your own.

When you begin to understand that there's something beyond your human that's always guiding you—that there is energy and light guiding you and a higher intelligence that is inspiring your dreams and drawing you into something more, something greater—you will begin to understand so-called divine will, and you will allow it to work for you in your life.

There is a plan here. There is a reason for you being here. And truly, you cannot get this wrong. Your experience, here and now, can still be so much more fun, so much more joyful, and so much more magical than most of you allow. Begin to expand your awareness and perspective; begin to move your awareness beyond the idea that you are just this human. As you begin to perceive into the grander perspective of what's possible for you and begin to allow your light and energy to guide your way, trusting the journey—however unexpected—you will begin living as the powerful creator that you are and that you intended to be when you focused yourself into form.

Your human will never be able to fully comprehend it or be able to figure things out from its limited perspective, but you can feel the truth of this. Circumstances may not be logical or make sense at the time, but you can possess a knowingness within you that all is supremely well, and you will better sense what direction to take for each of your life's major crossroads. They will become choiceless. Your life will feel easier and more effortless than it ever has before.

Does that mean that the ultimate life approach to "win" might be simply to learn how to surrender?

Indeed, but we'll continue to expand on this because we think it will be helpful.

Most of you would say, "But how do I surrender when there are things I really want? If I surrender, I might not get what I want." What you are saying is that you need to be in control of every moment of your life. You thereby limit what's possible for you. In this paradigm, there is a chance that you may find yourself later in life looking at your scorecard and thinking, "I failed. I didn't manifest all that I wanted." Even if you succeeded in creating far more things that you did desire, "the game" is not over (nor will it ever be).

How might you have experienced even more, sooner? By fully opening to all that you are and letting the Source energy and the God consciousness that you are be what guides and lights the way for you. This is the energy that creates worlds, and it is the energy that creates your world.

You say, "Well, I really want that." The order is still being processed! Meanwhile, "divine will" is aware of potentials and possibilities that are bigger and bolder and brighter and more expansive that not only include what you are now wanting, but all else you have ever wanted. There are potential manifestations that your human cannot even imagine. We're not saying don't pursue your dreams; we're saying to follow the energy and light to enable their fastest, greatest, most harmonious arrival—*or better!*

As you allow yourself into these higher levels of consciousness, you will begin to see that life will become easy and effortless. There will be more magic and miracles, wonderful manifestations beyond your wildest dreams will come to you out of the blue, and you will begin to recognize that your human alone couldn't have possibly created all of it. You will become aware that your human is limited and, in this, begin to perceive more of what's possible for you.

Since you used the word win, we would ask you, "Did you love it? Was it joyful? Was it fun? Did you play? Did you create? Did you create each moment of your reality the way you wanted to experience it?" That is winning. You are creating in every moment, and if you are reading this, there is something inside of you that remembers this. Your life can be abundant, prosperous, and rich in every way; you can create beauty and vitality and well-being, and you can create a wealth of everything, including resources, people, and experiences. You can flourish in every way and experience the highest vibrations and the highest feelings of joy, harmony, love, well-being, abundance, and freedom. And while you are creating this for yourself, you are also positively contributing to the raising of consciousness within the human collective, knowing that you're living your purpose in every moment.

Will you speak more on fulfillment and "purpose"?

When asked, "What is my purpose?" we respond, "What do you most want?" Is it peace, or freedom, or love, or joy, or beauty, or wealth, or abundance? Or is it a combination of these? Whatever it might be, your purpose in every moment is to bring yourself into that state, and in doing so the world around you will reflect that back to you.

Your purpose is to create your reality the way you want it to be. And we say to this end: divine will, which again is your soul's or higher self's grand plan, is here and available to you, and it is unfolding in a way that you can feel it, align to it, tune in to it.

Your next best step may not be logical; you might have to change some things, you might have to end some things, but there's something inside of you that knows you're either going with the energy and light that's guiding you, or you are resisting it, denying it, or doubting it because you think you must manage everyone else's behavior. Thereby unknowingly holding yourself apart from the reality you wanted to create, feeling the heaviness and density you were not meant to bear.

We know that none of you would intentionally create disease or disharmony in the body, in your relationships, or in your life. However, these things happen when you are denying the Source energy that you are. When you go against your own divine will, you will experience struggle.

Divine will is within you; it's a part of you, and it's always leading you and guiding you. It will never let you down. It will never disappoint.

The majority of you only feel like you're winning when you're fulfilling the responsibilities and expectations that you and everyone else, including your family, friends, coworkers, boss, and society, have placed on you. Yet, in the moment that you take full and total responsibility—without exception—for being the creator within your own creation, you will be free, and you will begin to create your reality the way you want it to be, as the master that you are. And you will know that it is and has all been perfect—that everything has always been happening *for* you, that everything is your creation within your own reality, and that nothing has gone wrong; there have been no mistakes, you didn't lose anything, really, and you didn't fail.

In the moment that you take full and total responsibility, you will realize that nothing is happening or has ever happened *to* you; all your creations were simply a reflection of your beliefs, your stories, your thoughts, and your level of consciousness at the time. And in this moment of freedom, you will no longer see life as navigating through change, you will see that you are, and have always been, navigating through creation. And if you choose to navigate through creation with the same people, you will likely create and re-create in a far more loving, harmonious, conscious, intentional way.

Ultimately, everyone wins because every experience you have provides data and information that leads to greater expansion and expression and that provides clarity for choosing more of the experiences that you want to have for you, as creator within your own creation.

THE ILLUSION OF DEATH, THE HUMAN EXPERIENCE, AND UNDERSTANDING ADVERSITY

When you said, "The order is still being processed," do some dreams of ours in this lifetime come to pass in the next? Related to that, what can you say about reincarnation?

Indeed. All dreams come true, as long as the wish remains.

One of the greatest illusions on your planet is the illusion of death. First, there is the fear of death—your own or that of a loved one—and the grieving that often comes with it. Then, for some, there is the concern about whether a person is in Heaven or Hell.

As we've said, nothing and no one ever dies. Everything is a continuation, an expansion. When you release the density of the body to continue your journey in the formless, you are still absolutely aware of the personality that you know as you. And you journey into more—into higher levels of consciousness and into grander experiences of yourself within this universe that is you.

Neither consciousness nor what you call your soul or spirit is limited to the body. These aspects of you exist eternally. The body itself returns to the Earth, where it dissolves and is re-created into something new. There is no death. There is no end; it is simply a continuation of the expansion, but in higher levels of consciousness. Not better levels of consciousness, just levels of consciousness where you're experiencing yourself more as Source energy.

When you focused your consciousness into physical form, you took on density. That's what allows you to move into form, and that's what allows you to play and create in form.

When someone releases the density of the body, they're in such a high rate of vibration and frequency that they cannot be perceived by the physical senses, unless a person in physical form is tuning themselves in to higher dimensions of consciousness.

Now to your question about reincarnation. From the human perspective, indeed you focus the consciousness that you are into physical form on Earth, and you experience yourself as a particular personality. Then, when your lifetime objectives have been met, or can no longer be met, as you judge to be the case, you release the density of the body.

In time, you may choose to focus yourself again into the human experience. Some beings never choose the human experience. Some have chosen to be here numerous times. Others are only now choosing to be physical for the first time.

Here's where we want to boggle your minds, just for the fun of it.

Again, all things are happening now. Because you are perceiving yourself as the human you know as you, you cannot fathom that you are currently and simultaneously focusing yourself into multiple different experiences. But this is what's going on: you are a multidimensional being, and this means simultaneously.

You are also creating everything in your reality. So, as you became curious about reincarnation and "past lives," you began to perceive yourself beyond this one physical life, where you know yourself as you, and into the experience of multiple lives and experiences, where you know yourself as more. Your interest and understanding of reincarnation were, and still may be, a very important part of the evolution of your consciousness.

At the time you were first exposed to the idea of reincarnation, you wouldn't have been able to perceive beyond that. But as you continue to expand your awareness and perceive yourself as more, you can then perceive yourself into more. Your curiosity moves you into an awareness of higher dimensions of consciousness where infinite potentials and possibilities and experiences exist, and that leads you to a grander perspective of all that you are and what's really going on. Then, as you allow these grander perspectives, you are allowing even more potentials, possibilities, and experiences.

Where an understanding of your multidimensional nature can help you—as the creator of your reality—is in addressing perceived harms. When you become aware of something terrible or awful that occurred in the past—either in your earlier experience of life or a "past life"—it is often a reflection of where you feel persecuted or victimized in some way in your current life experience. Too often, however, there's the feeling, "Well, that was the reality I experienced in the past. I can't change that. I was victimized." And that's where you stop wondering why you continue to re-create experiences of being victimized in your present-moment experiences. When you think of that situation as having happened in the past, you are limiting the way in which you can relate to it now. Instead, your awareness of a similar experience from a previous time can now allow you to work with your current situation; you can investigate the feeling of powerlessness or the idea of being a victim.

If you have an awareness of a past experience where you felt powerless or victimized, every timeline of potential for that experience is still available to you in this moment when you fully accept that you are creator within your own creation. So, if you want to bring that experience to a higher level, go into it in your imagination and create a new "reality" the way you choose it to be. Go back into that experience, but from where you are now. Instead of feeling helpless, stand in your power, say what is true for you now, and come into the knowing of the love, the light, the Source energy that you are and that they are. Re-create that event from the level of awareness and consciousness that you now have. By doing this, you are bringing light into that experience. You are elevating yourself and the experience into the highest level of consciousness, into the only truth of anything, which is love. This is not to change what happened, but to change how you feel about yourself and your ability to create your now moment and your future.

All "lives" are happening now, as is your past. And as you fully elevate your consciousness in one life experience, you are fully elevating it in every life experience. You can bring Source energy, God consciousness, and your truth into any life experience—past or present. Your awareness of this alone will help you recognize that everything in your experience is happening now. Then you can perceive yourself in any situation as the magnificent multidimensional being that you are, but fully aligned to truth, power, love, and consciousness.

We mean this with so much love, and the utmost compassion: we understand that many of you experienced highly traumatic events and emotional moments in your life. Because of the shock and the emotion of it, you have continued to re-create, unintentionally, of course, a reality where you are expressing the powerlessness that you felt in those moments, and you find yourself being victimized in your current life experiences.

We offer this with the greatest reverence and respect for you and for the courage it takes to come into this human experience knowing all that exists within lower dimensions of consciousness. You are not what happened to you. In this moment, you can choose a higher perspective and re-create that reality in any way you wish. In doing so, you will be creating new potentials for regaining and maintaining your power in all your situations and circumstances.

You can elevate your entire experience into levels of consciousness aligned solely to the truth of you, which is love. In those moments of realization, the past is completely healed and restored, and all experiences will have been returned to the light, re-created in love. This does not mean those prior events will be undone; it means they will be seen in the light of compassion, understanding, and unconditional love.

Many of you do not know who you are without that experience of what happened to you. So, if you are ready and can remember that that experience is not who you are, and that you have the power to come fully into this moment and tell a new story about it, you will transcend that experience and come to know yourself as God, as Source, as Divine, as Creator. And when you do, you will begin to direct your energy into literally creating a new reality for yourself, free from the past, bringing all your power, love, and consciousness into the now moment. Only choosing new timelines, realities, and experiences that you want to experience.

The second you go back and fight for your limitation—"Well, that really did happen to me, I was victimized, they did wrong me"—you are giving your energy, your focus, and your attention to that unwanted reality, keeping it active in your field of consciousness and vibration.

We'll tell you something else that might help. Every single one of you can create the reality you wish to experience. No matter who you are—or what you've done or experienced in your life that has resulted in pain—as you continue to elevate your consciousness and come more fully into the realization of who you are, the traumatic events of the past will cease to loom so large, if ever again. They will not be active in your vibration. It's like the analogy we gave you before of the staircase with many steps. As you realize more of the truth of you and others as love, the higher you will be on the staircase; and the experiences at the bottom of the staircase will have far less effect on you.

Imagine there is a terrible movie playing on a small television at the bottom of the stairs. The higher you go up the staircase, the less you can hear the movie. With each step, there's more peace, more harmony, maybe even a beautiful melody begins to play from somewhere else. Everything seems to get lighter, brighter, and easier; it's lovely and amazing. The further up you go on the staircase, the more incredible the view, and suddenly you can imagine so much more for yourself. You're going to be so satiated by these higher consciousness experiences that you're not going to want to turn around and walk back down those stairs to watch that terrible movie again.

Right. I get that. Yet for those who are still bitter, and understandably so . . .

Consider, again, when this lifetime is done and you release the density of the body, the pain and confusion of those experience will be replaced with joy and love, with an excitement over further adventures in new realms.

So, do you want to continue to drag any unhappy memories of yours along with you for the rest of this life experience, until you release the density of the body? Or would you now like to create your reality the way you want it to be?

Consider also, there are many things that have happened in the human experience that you would call "terrible," yet you have never known about them. However, because no one is talking about those events or labeling them as "awful," you don't even know they happened. So, are they reality? They're not your reality because you're not focused upon them and you're not giving them a particular meaning and experiencing a particular emotion that keeps those events active in your vibration.

So, if something "terrible" is happening right now in someone else's reality, is it your reality?

Only if you focus upon it and give it meaning in your reality is it part of your reality. The only thing that exists is this moment, and when those terrible things happened in the past, they only happened in those moments. All you have is the moment; *what you're focused on and giving meaning to now is what's creating your reality.* And that is the reality that you will be experiencing and perpetuating.

Is there potential to not focus on something that happened to you in the past, to not feel hurt or victimized? Of no longer focusing your attention on, or giving meaning to, that experience to remove it from your reality? Absolutely. That is available to you in any moment.

Some of you are very affected by stories about certain things that have happened, either because your families were involved or because of an emotional response to things you see in the news, books, movies, or the like. We will say this again because it is so very important and it's the reason you're here: *what you focus on and the meaning you're giving it is now creating your reality.*

It may be difficult to hear this, but we assure you, you drew this information to you because you wanted to remember your power so that you could begin creating your reality the way you want it to be.

The reason you often fight for your limitations, or the traumas and dramas of the past, is because you don't know who you would be without them. You've been focused for so long on that reality that you have no idea what your reality could be. And we assure you that a reality of more peace and joy and love and harmony and beauty and well-being and abundance and freedom is available to you now, and in every moment beyond if it is your choosing.

It does make sense. I'm sure this will challenge many, but we're here to expand our thinking about what's possible in our human experiences.

Here's a process that will help many:

First, come into a place of forgiveness.

Second, realize there's only love.

We don't talk a lot about forgiveness because the highest truth is that there is only love. You came from love, and love is what you are. This is the highest truth of all, regardless of how a person expresses themself in form.

Once you understand that there's only love, you can open yourself to see the love, the gifts, and the blessings that have come from each and every experience. This is forgiveness.

If you're still holding on to resentment, anger, hatred, rage, or another emotion, you will find that those emotions get triggered in you time and time again. Whether in your work, your relationships, or your life, including when you're driving down the street. You may not realize that the person cutting you off on the road is something that you created through your focus on an experience other than love, but that is what's happening.

We're going to say one more thing here. People tell us, "But the experience of being abused, the experience of prejudice, the experience of any of those things, those are not of love." And they ask, "Where is God in all of those things?"

We understand why you would think this way, but the God spark is within everyone. We want you to understand that when someone hurts or harms or abuses another, they have completely forgotten the truth of who they are. They are in such low vibrational density and in such an experience of separation that they're choosing to create a reality that causes pain and harm and struggle and suffering—first and foremost to themselves and then to those around them. And yet everyone is Source, an aspect of the Divine.

It is understood on a soul level that occurrences such as these happen in lower dimensions of consciousness, where the tendency has been, for a very long time, to perpetuate separation and, therefore, pain and suffering. But you are here now, as we've said, for the greatest awakening that humanity has ever experienced. More of you than ever before are seeing the truth that you and all others are love, Source, God, the Divine.

When you understand and see things from this perspective, this awareness, you can really begin to see all of it from a much higher vantage point, without any judgment of right or wrong. And when you can see without any judgment of right or wrong, you will not entangle with the struggle and the suffering and the abuse and the harm and the pain and the fear that occurs when one is in a lower dimension of consciousness.

Every single one of you can open to a level of God force and Source energy where you experience a reality of love, joy, peace, and harmony everywhere you go, with everyone you meet, in every interaction you have. It's about what you focus on and the meaning you're giving it.

Let's say you come together with a group of friends, and one of them starts talking about a person and how terrible they are. They begin describing the dreadful things the person did and how it is affecting them. As your friend is speaking, you begin to get a holographic image in your mind of the terribleness of the other person and may even begin to feel some emotion related to it. Suddenly, you hear yourself thinking, or saying out loud, "Oh, that's awful; they are terrible to treat others that way." So, you begin judging the terribleness of that other person. Then, suddenly, you start remembering all the other awful and terrible people you know who have done similar things, and even all the awful and terrible things happening in the world. This is what we mean by entangled. Through your attention and focus on the terribleness, you have instantly brought this lower-level vibration into your present-moment experience. The result? You feel terrible.

If you step back and look at the situation, there was a moment—in fact many moments—where you could have exercised free will and chosen to stay conscious, present, and aligned to the truth of who you are, to not entangle through judging another, and you could have stayed in the truth that everyone is Source, God, the Divine. Indeed, then you could have incredible compassion without entangling.

By focusing on compassion, you'd find very little interest in pointing out and focusing upon the "wrongs" of the world, as that would be re-creating those wrongs and the suffering that comes with them through your focus and attention. Thus, you are keeping them alive in your field of consciousness, as well as in the collective consciousness. Instead, if you want to create a world where there is more peace, more joy, more harmony, more love, more abundance, more freedom, and more well-being, you do it by going higher. Focus on the higher perspective with forgiveness and love.

Really understand this: you are creator within your own creation. As you create what you want within you, you positively contribute to new potentials and possibilities in the world around you. If you want to see a peaceful, joyful, harmonious, abundant world where all experience love and well-being and freedom, create it first within you. As you take full responsibility for what you are creating, you can choose moment by moment: Do you want to focus on and give meaning to the unwanted, or do you want to focus on and give meaning to that which you want? Whatever you choose, that is the reality you are creating. This is how powerful you are.

Can we get more details on exactly what happens when someone dies? They release the density of their physical body, and then what?

We'd first like to give you the highest perspective of what this experience can be for you and all who choose it. The experience of focusing yourself into a physical body requires much more attention and energy than releasing the density of the body and experiencing what you call death, although there is no such thing.

The highest perspective is that you can live your magnificent life experience at the highest levels of joy, peace, love, harmony, abundance, freedom, and well-being. And you can live at such a high level of vibration and consciousness, until the moment of transition, where you barely notice that you've released the density of the body. How do you know you're ready? You would feel an inspiration, a calling to yet another adventure, another exciting and new adventure. And without any fear—feeling only peace, harmony, love, and joy—you would have the awareness of beginning to release the density of the body and making your transition from physical into nonphysical. With this high level of consciousness, instead of grieving it, pushing against it, or resisting it, you would embrace and celebrate it. You would find the deepest moments of love and appreciation for life, for everything in your life, for everyone in your life, and for all that you had experienced. And in that moment of absolute fullness, you would release your body to the Earth, taking one last breath, in absolute peace and harmony. You would then come into realization in the formless, beyond the physical, to continue your journey.

Each of you can choose in this lifetime how you will one day release the body when your journey here is complete. You need not entangle with decay, disease, pain, struggle, or suffering. Instead, you can make your transition in a way that is peaceful and harmonious, knowing that you will be continuing on to your next adventure having great appreciation for the life you just lived.

No matter how anyone chooses to leave this incarnation, in the moment they take their final breath, release the density of the body, and consciousness moves from physical into nonphysical, there is absolute peace and pure bliss—absolute knowing that there is only love. Most people are unaware they can choose how they make their transition, let alone believe in their power to create such a thing. And most have such high levels of resistance to and fear about death that they—unconsciously, of course, because we know that no one would intentionally choose it—create the experience of a painful or horrible death through disease or disability. When you do not remember the truth of who you are, what's going on, and what's possible, it's easy to entangle with disease as a way of leaving this incarnation.

Much of this pattern has to do with humanity's current level of consciousness about death. Most, feeling the urge to release the body and move into higher dimensions of consciousness, would go into resistance and fear. Then if they were to tell anyone—close family and friends—that they were feeling called to leave the planet and move into a new experience, they would likely be met with despair, grief, anger, frustration, torment, pain, and suffering.

Those of you reading or hearing this information will choose differently because you have the awareness of a new potential. And as you choose a harmonious, peaceful, empowered way of releasing the body and continuing your journey, you will be showing your human family a new way. Then, in just a few generations, the pattern of how humans make their transitions will have shifted. This, incidentally, is how you'll eradicate deadly diseases on your planet.

We hear from people who have had near-death experiences that they undergo a life review and sometimes receive guidance. What can you tell us about this? Also, do we all have the choice to remain in the afterlife or to come back?

Indeed. It's always a choice.

What would be some of the standard, routine elements of one's transition?

People having a near-death experience still have consciousness, though one that is not limited to the body. There is still awareness and a knowing of who you are. And there is a tremendous love and light because of the vibration and frequency you experience beyond the density of the physical body.

For these reasons, many would choose to stay, and yet in some instances there is a grander awareness offered by what you would call guides, your higher or God self that encourages the person to return with an awareness of the higher level of consciousness and light they're now experiencing. Many have full-on awakening, enlightenment experiences because of this. Always, however, it's their own choosing.

While this describes a near-death experience, one needn't wait to experience the incredible feeling of the light and the awareness of who they really are. This is our main teaching. Anyone choosing to be on the planet at this time can come fully into enlightenment and embody the master that they are while still in form.

It bears repeating, for countless centuries and generations, those who first came into enlightenment, prior to their transition, chose to almost instantly leave their body and move into the formless. Yet at this particular time on Earth, you are asked—or better said, you chose, even though you may not remember—to come into this incarnation to realize the truth of who you are, and to live as the master that you are, fully enlightened, while fully embodied.

Being a master does not mean sitting on a mountaintop and meditating every day. It's about creating your reality the way you want it to be and living your life to the fullest—loving fully and being all that you are. Living your bliss while positively contributing to raising the consciousness and vibration on the planet and seeding humanity with new potentials and possibilities for the human experience.

This is the dream; this is your dream, and it's why you've chosen to be here. You've drawn this information to you so you could remember. There's something within you right now that knows this, even as you may be saying, "I am not a master. I'm not ready to be a master. How can I be a master?" We assure you, our friend, if you drew this book to you, you are, indeed, a master. Not a master over any other. Being a master in human form simply means living as a realized being: you realize yourself as more than just human; you realize yourself as All That Is, as Source, as God, as Light, as the Divine, and you realize the dream in your heart for Heaven on Earth—for peace, for joy, for love, for harmony, for well-being, for abundance, for beauty and freedom for all. Realization is the embodiment of all that you are, and it is your reason for being here now.

Neither is the world's perfection required. The instant you begin focusing on fixing or changing it, you're entangling with lack and limitation; you're back in separation and in lower levels of consciousness, which will only give you more experiences of lack and limitation and separation.

You come into realization because you want to experience living your highest potential in this human experience, and because you want to experience the highest levels of abundance, well-being, love, joy, prosperity, freedom, beauty, harmony, and peace. You come into realization to enjoy this experience more than you could have ever imagined before. When you embody your realization, people will come to you, they will watch you, they will see that you're doing "life" differently, they will see that you're living beyond limitation and lack and separation, they will see the magnificent circumstances that come to you out of the blue, they will see you creating magic and miracles, and they will see that you're living at the highest levels of abundance and well-being and love and joy and prosperity and freedom and beauty and harmony and peace. They will know that all of this is somewhere within them, that it's possible for them, too. And this serves in ways that your human will never understand.

REALIZATION, FOCUS, AND HEAVEN ON EARTH

Has *everyone* come here now to realize? Or are some just here for the experience—the grandiosity of all the emotions, the journeys, the highs, the lows, the beauty, the power, and the fear?

All of you are here for the human experience, to be part of this grand experiment in physical form. All are here to create in physical form, in this density, in this so-called "plane of demonstration" within the human experience.

You're here to explore all that's part of this adventure. And as you explore, you expand. Even those that you identify as not realized, or having no interest in realization, contribute to the expansion of consciousness. They contribute to the evolution by creating and expressing themselves and through the experiences they have. Someone does not have to be realized to contribute. However, if you drew this information to you, this is the lifetime you've chosen to come fully into realization.

We don't want you to make this difficult. It's not a test and you cannot fail. And as we said before, this experience is meant to be so very fun. You're here to play and create and enjoy and evolve and expand and come deeper into the realization of all that you are along the way. There is no rush. There is no deadline. There is really nothing to do. In fact, it's more of an undoing: see beyond the illusions, see all that you are, and allow all that you are into every experience; that is living as a realized master. Nothing outside of you is passing judgment. Nothing outside is putting pressure on you to "learn lessons." These are just beliefs that you have practiced for a very long time. If you believe you're being tested, you will continually draw experiences into your reality that feel like tests. If you believe you're here to learn lessons, you will continue to draw lessons.

It really is quite simple: your free will choices determine your experiences here in form. What is it that you want to experience more of? Is it peace and freedom and joy, or is it struggle and limitation and effort? You are the creator within your own creation; you get to choose.

You could look at some in your human experience and say, "Well, they are winning the game. They have a lot of influence, power, and money; they are successful." Yet if their highest potential in this life was not fame or fortune or wealth and was instead realization, are they really winning at the game? Many have come into realization through what you call success, but others that you would say are successful haven't realized because of the expectations they impose upon their human in this experience—expectations that distract them from realization.

I have heard you say that we as humans haven't even scratched the surface of how good things will get. Might you give us a sneak peek of how good life can be for us once we move into Heaven

on Earth, the New Earth that we seem now to be on the cusp of?

We have asked countless people what their perfect day would look like, be like. And without exception they all give us some variation of the same answer:

I would wake up feeling energized, vital, and inspired and excited about my life. Upon rising, I would do something that I love to do; I would meditate or visualize or exercise or read or play with my children and animals or spend time in nature. I would take some time to be with myself and focus on what it is that I wanted to create and experience that day. I'd have a delicious, beautiful meal that nourishes my body. Then I would move into an activity or a project or a creation or a service that inspired and excited me—where I would tune in to Source energy and the inspiration and creativity would flow through me.

I would create something wonderful and do what I love, and I would share it with the world. And then I would do the playful, fun things I enjoy. I would spend time with the people I love the most; I would dance and sing and laugh. And throughout my day I would look for the highest perspectives, the highest levels of well-being, and the highest levels of abundance that would inspire me to do the things I wanted to do. I would have all the resources I needed to create my day in the highest, most inspired way. I would feel great within my body, and my relationships would be loving and harmonious and conscious. I would continue to expand and be inspired and explore new things and come into new levels of awareness. I would see the beauty in everything around me: in my home, in nature, and in all the people that I saw that day.

I would have experiences of new things that excited me and delighted me and expanded me. Then I would watch the beautiful sunset. After nightfall I'd look at the stars, and I would end my day feeling like I had lived it to the fullest—so grateful, so happy, so thankful, so full and fulfilled by my life, and so full of love. And then, when I was so completely full and so completely savoring all that I experienced that day, I would close my eyes to rest and restore and re-create the next perfect day, and the next.

That is the greatest vision we could give you.

What a beautiful vision. And I believe you would also tell us that we can choose that existence right now.

Indeed. And many of you are.

I suppose that more of us will be choosing that, while supporting each other to do the same.

Your next question might be this: What if I choose this for myself, but there are people around me choosing struggle, suffering, disharmony, chaos, poverty, lack, and limitation? How can I live my perfect day each day when others aren't living this way? And how can my perfect days be my reality if that's not the reality that everyone else, including loved ones, is experiencing?

You are creator within your own creation. What you focus on and the meaning you give it is what is creating your reality. If you began to hold such a truth—knowing that Heaven on Earth is here for you now, and that the Heaven on Earth state of consciousness is available to you and everyone here and now—you will create a reality that reflects that back to you. As you choose this reality for yourself, you simply would not see or focus upon or distract yourself with that which is not in your creation of reality.

The ultimate distraction within the human experience is the idea or belief that you must manage, control, and choose for others. You think that you need to get everyone else to want what you want, and do what you're doing, so that you can have the life you want. And it simply doesn't work that way.

What if somebody felt so aligned with what you are saying, but at the same time, they fear that just living in their own little happy-go-lucky bubble of joy isn't enough in these challenging times. What would you say to the people who are choosing to not give their attention to the divisiveness or the polarity that is tearing communities and nations apart right now and who, as a result, might also feel they're neglecting important social issues that may be a threat to their existence? Might it be a better idea to be in both worlds? Be in your bubble of joy but at the same time carry some picket signs, promote a candidate, let your views be heard, and stay informed? Is there some chance that we could lose control of our lives if we just got wrapped up into our little bubble of joy?

As we've said, what you focus on and the meaning you are giving it is what is creating your reality. You are voting with your attention. So, if you're focused on war, on crime, and on all the wrongdoings in the world, that's what you're giving your energy to. Source energy is flowing through you, and you are directing it—through your focus—to war, to crime, and to wrongdoings.

Just as you cannot get sick enough to make a sick person well, you also cannot focus on a person's sickness to make them well. The same goes for all the sickness of the world. It doesn't work to focus on all of those who are sick and think that somehow, they will become well. Whatever it is, war, crime, wrongdoings, or sickness occur because a person or a group of people have forgotten who they are.

What you're really saying to us is: I know the truth of who I am—as Source, as God consciousness, as Light, as the Divine—and I've come into a state of consciousness where I realize the power within me, the creator that I am within my own creation. But because so many others are living in an illusion, when I'm around them, I'm going to choose to focus myself into their reality instead of mine.

Most of you would recognize that it doesn't feel very good to do this. It doesn't feel good to live someone else's reality, especially when it's not in alignment with yours. We are not saying that you will not be inspired to do great things with love that have a tremendous impact in the world, but what you're really asking is, should I lower my consciousness, my vibration by participating in the illusion of separation, of war, of chaos, of judgment, of disagreement, of death, and of right and wrong? Should I participate for the sake of saving the world because so many believe in the illusion that it needs to be saved? We tell you that this would not be honoring the truth of you or them or what's going on here.

We know the dream in your heart, and we know how much each of you wants to help. Help by choosing to elevate your consciousness into your truth. By doing this, you are contributing to the elevation of consciousness within all of humanity and creating a path toward love, peace, harmony, and well-being for all. The truth of you is love.

The truth of all others is love. The truth of everything is love. You are an extension of Source energy; that is the truth of who you are; that is the truth of who all others are too, and that is the truth within all things.

Stand in your power, stand in your truth, and hold your consciousness and vibration in that level of consciousness, no matter who you're with, no matter what others are doing, or what's going on in the news or around you. Do not forget the truth of you, and do not focus yourself into an illusion.

You are so powerful when you stand in your truth, fully open to the Source energy, the God consciousness that flows through you. If there was fighting going on around you and you walked into a room, fully allowing that power, that Source energy that is you, holding your awareness and your focus on the truth of you and everyone in front of you, there would be such an intense frequency of peace and love that the fighting would end. And it wouldn't matter to you that anyone had any awareness that you had something to do with it; you would know the power that you have. And you weren't doing that to change anything. You didn't do it because you judged them and their fighting as wrong. You did it because the truth of you is peace and harmony and well-being. And in the powerful, focused alignment to that state of consciousness, in that moment all others would remember the truth within themselves too.

You can get so good at this that you can walk by a television that has what you would have previously called "terrible things" going on and it would not affect you. You can stay in such a level of consciousness and awareness that you see and don't judge the illusion. You just know that *there is only love*. That is when you can allow others to be where they are on their journey through different levels of consciousness and experiences within this human existence.

Would that be an example of the law of resonance, where a person of serene peace and truth–call it enlightenment–could still or calm the energy of a room into which they walk? Is there more to say about that?

There are many laws, but we prefer the phrase *your truth*. The truth is that you're a vibrational being. The truth is that you bring your vibration and a frequency everywhere you go. The truth is that your vibration and frequency are not limited to your body, because you are a force field of consciousness. The more expanded your force field becomes, through the elevation of your consciousness, vibration, and frequency, the more energy you summon to move manifestation and creation into form.

You may be sitting in your home, powerfully focusing yourself into a state of consciousness of absolute peace and harmony, well-being and freedom, abundance, and love. From there, you could focus yourself even higher, into the God consciousness that you are and that's always available to you. Then, for as far as you can see or imagine, in that moment there would be peacefulness. The peacefulness didn't come from your human. What you did was focus your human into such a vibration where you were fully allowing Source energy and God consciousness to flow through you into the physical experience.

This is when the magic and miracles occur. It's not because you're trying to change or fix things; it's simply because you're coming into the truth of you and allowing it into your experience. You're elevating your vibration and your consciousness and your frequency into alignment with Source energy and letting that energy flow through you.

The more fully you allow the light, the love, the Source energy, the God consciousness that you are, and the more frequently you go beyond the things that trigger you, that trip you up, and that keep you from fully expressing the light within you, the more powerful you become. As we say, *one of you in your power is more powerful than millions who are not.* Remember, it's not power over them, but power with them so that they, too, can remember the dream in their heart.

Concerning resonance, everything has a vibration. So, when you come into proximity with another person or place, including places in nature, whether conscious of it or not, your vibrations are always seeking to resonate. You may walk into a room and you're happy and feeling good but notice that another person in the room has their head down. You can tell they're upset. What you're recognizing is their vibration or frequency. And if you're unaware of the fact that your vibrations are seeking to resonate, you can tend to lower yours in an attempt to meet that person where they are.

Just being aware of this will allow you to stay conscious and not go into an unconscious reaction. To stay conscious in the moment, breathe, and stay present to the truth of you and the truth of them. Stay connected to your power. Be in the highest vibration possible for you in that moment. You are not trying to change them; you are simply staying aware of and present to the higher level of consciousness.

If you do this with absolute love in your heart, absolute acceptance of what is, and if you stay in the moment, stay in your power, and be present with them, they will begin to feel their way into a higher vibrational frequency. Again, you're not trying to change them, and you're not doing it because you're right and they're wrong. You're doing it because you're being the powerful creator of your creation; you're embodying the truth of who you are—as love, as beauty, as freedom, as well-being, as abundance, as peace. This is an example of you living the dream in your heart. And as you live this dream, you are making it easier for another to choose to do the same. And that, dear friends, is why we call you wayshowers; it is why you are here.

You are very important. You chose to focus yourself into a human body at this time—during the greatest awakening of humanity in any lifetime. You did this because of your great love for humanity, for Earth, and for all its inhabitants. You came here to first remember the dream in your heart and then to live it. Because in the living of it you are seeding humanity with new potentials and possibilities that will forever change the human experience and what is possible in this experience. This is how important you are.

SECTION 3

THE JOURNEY

In this section, The Council explores how to wisely navigate our dreams, our experiences, and the challenges between birth and death.

How do we live up to our highest potential? How do we best navigate the things that happen, the things we want to happen, the things that don't happen, and how do we interact with all the potentials and possibilities that lie within it—the journey through our days.

Ultimately your highest potential is to come into the realization that you are creator within your own creation of reality. Your highest potential, therefore, is to embody and live those things that you most value and want to experience more of—the joy, peace, love, harmony, abundance, well-being, freedom, beauty, fun, adventure, inspiration, creativity—to embody that and live that and to create your reality the way you wish it to be. To elevate your consciousness and your awareness to a state of what we call Heaven on Earth; in this state, anything and everything within the human experience is possible for you. In reaching these levels of consciousness, you will expand the potentials and possibilities for you and for all your human family within the human experience.

Let us simplify it for you. In every moment, you're either choosing fear or you're choosing love. Which is your highest potential? Love. The same question applies to lack or abundance. Which do you think is your highest potential? Which would you choose? Of course, you would say abundance. And finally, we'll ask you about struggle and bondage or freedom? Which do you think is your highest potential? Which would you choose? And you would say freedom.

You all know the highest potentials—freedom, joy, love, peace, harmony, well-being, abundance, beauty, fun. But your thoughts, and your perceptions about your reality, and your beliefs about yourself and what is possible distract you from these higher states of consciousness. Many of you are doubting and denying your highest potential instead of simply allowing it. Most of you have awareness of the untrue stories—based on lack and limitation—you tell about yourself, your life, and what's possible for you. These stories are not the truth of you, but because you've been telling them for decades, you think they're true. If your stories were true, then your highest potential would be lack and limitation, but you know your highest potential is abundance, prosperity, freedom, and well-being. You are the one who chooses the stories.

Your highest potential is also knowing that you have infinite resources and Source energy—the energy that creates worlds—available to you at all times. While that energy can create worlds, it is also the energy that creates your world, your life, your experience the way you want it to be.

When you're open to that energy, and allowing it, anything and everything is possible for you. When you're doubting and denying that energy, you experience lack, limitation, fear, separation, struggle, suffering, poverty, disease, despair—all of these and more.

Failure is a creation of the human, but so is success. If you were to ask us what success looks like in the human experience, we again remind you it's your level of joy. How much joy are you experiencing in every area of your life? Many in your experience are considered successful because they have fame and lots of money, yet they are not joyful in their work, their life, or their relationships. They don't feel a sense of freedom. They don't have loving relationships. They have disharmony in their body. In terms of your highest potential: how much joy you feel determines how much success you'll meet.

There is no true failure from our perspective. Failure is an illusion. Every one of your experiences provides data and information that leads to your expansion. Furthermore, there is no experience that is happening to you. Everything is happening *for* you. And taking it one step further, everything is happening *of* you.

Let us explain. In your journey, through different levels of consciousness within the human experience, there are times where you experience unwanted circumstances and situations. We know you would never consciously or intentionally create a disease, debt, a loss of money or business, a terrible fall, destruction or suffering of any kind. But as creator within your own creation, you can draw these experiences to you through an unconscious focus on lack and limitation in some area of your life. Because we know the truth of you as creator within your own creation, as Source energy, God consciousness, the Divine, we can only ever say that nothing is happening to you. Yet your belief in this illusion keeps so many trapped in powerlessness.

You're here for your expansion, and all experiences serve in this. Everything is happening for you. It is happening for your expansion, the expansion of your consciousness, for your highest potential. As you accept this, you will be able to find the peace and perfection in all things. There would be less fear, less struggle, less lack and limitation, and less separation between you and your experiences.

Finally, as you elevate your consciousness by knowing that nothing is happening to you and everything is happening for you, you can then begin to know and experience yourself as creator within your own creation. You come into a very high level of awareness, where you take full and total responsibility for yourself as creator of your reality. From this perspective, you will know absolutely what we know, which is that everything is happening for you.

As you move yourself into a much more expanded experience of what is possible for you and what is possible within all of creation, you would no longer judge what you may have previously called "terrible" or "bad" or "awful." Instead, you would come into the level of consciousness of pure love, of oneness consciousness, of unity consciousness, and you would see the perfection in it all. So, whether it's disease, debt, a loss of money or business, the death of a loved one, or some experience like this, you would experience it from the level of truth that we just described, and you would not entangle with the heavy and dense thoughts and emotional reactions that may have previously moved you into extreme grief or shame for long periods of time.

What are your tips for rocking our lives, and, as you just defined, for living at the highest levels of joy?

From the highest level of consciousness, you get more of what you are, not more of what you want. So, as you focus on joy, and do the things that bring you joy, and feel joyful, you will get even more joy. And as you practice this over time, you will find that you don't even remember a time in your life when you weren't joyful. You'd be so focused on joy, choosing joy, doing things that bring you joy, in a vibration of joy, and getting more of what you are—joy.

Indeed. There is only one tip, really:

Do what brings you joy!

Be in joy, focus on joy, feel the joy, live in joy, and you will only continue to attract more and more joy.

Now, some of you have asked, "Can I be in joy even when I'm experiencing the transition or the loss of a loved one? I am feeling some sadness that they won't be here much longer or are no longer in physical form." Our answer to them is that in staying fully conscious and present with the human experience of sadness in the moment it arises, you will still feel the joy. This is you choosing joy—by not making yourself or your experience wrong, by not going into stories that cause pain, and by allowing the love and peace and well-being that is always available to you. You can stay conscious and present and aware in any situation without losing your joy.

We understand that there's some parts of the human experience that because of the love that you have for certain people, animals, and places, when they change form there is a feeling of loss and sadness. Understand, this stems from the story you're telling yourself. Your beliefs are creating an emotional response of sadness within the body.

Here is one scenario. Let's say your loved one is sitting in the room with you; you feel so much love for them, and you're having such a wonderful time. Then they tell you that they are going somewhere wonderful and important, so they depart. You know that they're only going to be gone for a couple of minutes, a couple of hours, or a couple of days. For this reason, you probably wouldn't feel sadness about that. Let's say that they don't even leave the house. Instead, they tell you they're going into the other room, but you cannot see them or hear them; they just aren't in the room with you anymore. You would not be in grief, and you would not feel deep sadness; nor would you flounder in pain, or suffer, or struggle while they're away from you. Why? Because your story is that they're absolutely fine; they just stepped away, they'll soon be coming back, and you'll see them again.

But when someone makes their transition, leaves the physical body, and moves into the nonphysical, the story often changes. "Oh, they're gone!" and you start telling a story that they're "dead," and that you will never see them again, and how awful it is that you can't feel them, touch them, or talk to them anymore. You believe new opportunities have been lost forever, that they weren't ready, were too young, and had so much to look forward to that will now never be possible. With this story, you move yourself into a reality of deep sadness, loss, grief, and pain. And you find yourself at the bottom of the staircase.

Meanwhile, your dearly departed loved one is now more in the room with you after their passing than ever before. But you are so used to focusing on them with your physical senses that you miss what's still available to you in the higher dimensions of consciousness, where they can still be reached, and their well-being is assured.

We understand that you so love the personalities of the beings with whom you experience this incarnation. We understand that as they continue their journey into higher levels of consciousness it's not the same, that nothing will ever be the same. However, energy is never destroyed; it is only ever-changing form. So, when you can find some level of acceptance and go to a higher perspective concerning their transition and what's possible for you because of it—greater levels of love and expansion—you may observe some moments of sadness within your human, but you will not lose your joy.

FAST MANIFESTING AND LEVELS OF CONSCIOUSNESS

This is very profound. Thank you so much. I'd like to move to another topic: manifesting. As you know, there was a very popular book and movie called *The Secret*. It was about the Law of Attraction. In alignment with that, I'd like to ask you, from your perspective, what is the secret to better, happier, faster manifesting?

Consciousness. The answer is consciousness. Again, the formula for creation is: consciousness moves energy into form. What was so wonderful about *The Secret* is that it brought a level of awareness to humanity that how you feel opens you up to more of the same energy.

The next evolution of the Law of Attraction is True Creation. True Creation has no agenda. To create at this level, you simply elevate your consciousness to fully allow the Source energy that you are into your life, and it will take endless exciting, surprising, incredible forms. Consciousness moves energy into form, and it can move unlimited light and love into your life.

For many people today, when they talk about manifestation, their motivation comes from avoiding unwanted circumstances or fear.

They are in fear. They are in lack and limitation. They are in the struggle and suffering. "I don't want to run out of money. I don't want to fail my family, my children. I don't want to be a disappointment in society. I don't want to get sick. I don't want to lose my job. I don't want to be alone. I don't want . . ." and the list goes on and on. And then they say to themself, "I'd better go out there, and push and force and effort, make something happen, and figure this all out." It's all to avoid the unwanted, yet they don't realize their entire focus is on the unwanted. So, as powerful creators in their own creation, the particles of infinite creation continue to organize in their reality as more unwanted experiences.

At this point, they may ask the question, "Who am I?"—realizing that they don't have the same motivations anymore or that nothing exciting motivates them. They don't have the life they want, and they don't know how to create through joy.

The human experience is a journey through different dimensions of consciousness, and it is within the 5th Dimension that you begin to move into True Creation. As we said earlier, the 3rd Dimension is the dimension of separation. The 4th Dimension is the dimension of transformation. And the 5th Dimension is the dimension of pure love; in this dimension your well-being and abundance is assured. Here, whatever you want and need shows up, even before you know you need it, and it's where you know everything's being divinely orchestrated for you.

In the 5th Dimension, you follow the energy and let the light guide the way, and you fully open to and allow Source energy to flow through you. You fully allow the God consciousness within you, without doubting or denying your power to create your world and your reality as you wish it to be. And in your expansion, new potentials and possibilities present themselves to you; things just begin to show up for you out of the blue. You no longer experience lack, limitation, delay, or fear. Things show up that excite you and delight you, because you're living in such a state of alignment, and in such a high level of consciousness.

This is where you and our readers are going now. You're going beyond the desire to manifest something out there because of the lack, limitation, fear, not-enoughness, and separation that you're feeling inside of yourself. The next evolution of creation is about you coming into absolute fullness and wholeness, into your alignment with joy, love, abundance, well-being, happiness, freedom, beauty, and richness.

Then you won't experience long periods of waiting or trying to be patient, or trying to figure it out, or trying to make it happen, and trying to push and force energy where you think it should go.

There are no "wrong" manifestations, and there's never judgment from our side about your manifestations. However, your manifestations are either in alignment with the truth of you, which is love, abundance, well-being, harmony, happiness, joy, freedom, beauty, inspiration, and creativity, or they are in alignment with some perceived idea of lack or limitation. Yet manifesting can still work even then—that is how powerful you are.

Let's say you are in a situation where you do not have the money you think you need or want in this Earthly existence, because we recognize you need money in your world, and you start to look around you and think, "Well, those people have more money than I do; if I had that amount of money, then I would be happy." You are sitting there in a vibration of lack, thinking you have to go out there and get it, that you have to bring it to you, or chase the money down until you finally get it.

That is one way of getting what you want in lower dimensions of consciousness. However, because you never aligned with the state of abundance, even if you get the money, or whatever it is you're pursuing, you're very likely to continue experiencing lack and limitation. You will find yourself constantly chasing after something outside of you, and you will never feel the freedom, abundance, and well-being that you thought you would once you got what you thought you wanted.

We said to you at the beginning of this journey together, "Everything you wish to be, you already are." Align to this and create from there. Then your creations and manifestations will be coming from the highest levels.

Can you further explain how we learn to "follow the energy"? And how do we "open and allow"?

When you find yourself in a situation where you are trying to figure something out, attempting to fix something, or thinking you need to do something—and you're feeling some resistance around that—the easiest and best thing to do is to stop and ask, "What can I do right now that would bring me joy?"

Instead of trying to resolve the situation from an experience of lack, limitation, and struggle, or pushing and forcing yourself to find a solution, you want to bring yourself into a higher vibration; elevate your level of consciousness.

If you are aligned in your asking, and you let your awareness go into a place of inspiration, something will "light up"—a thought, a vision, or an idea will come. Then go do that thing. Because when you go do that thing that you love and that brings you joy, you're following the energy, you're following the light. You are no longer in the lower dimension of consciousness, forcing, efforting, and pushing energy where you think it should go. Whatever inspiration comes, it will feel joyful, it will be fun, and it will light you up.

You might think to yourself, "Well, you know, I'm actually hungry, so I'm going to go to that little deli that

I love and get a sandwich." So, you go to the deli and get your sandwich. You're sitting there enjoying it when suddenly someone you thought of the other day, someone you really like and haven't seen for a long time, walks into the same shop. Your friend gets their sandwich, sits down with you, and before long they are telling you a story that gives you an idea of how to resolve the situation that was troubling you earlier. That leads to the next thing, which leads to the next thing, and the next. That's following energy and letting light guide the way. That's an experience of true creation. You stopped forcing and started allowing through the simple act of following your joy.

Just ask yourself, what would feel good? What would bring me joy? What would I love to do? What would be fun? And let it come to you. Most of the time you do not realize that your answers to these types of questions do not come from your thinking mind or your brain—they're inspired. This is the energy you permit yourself to receive when you open and allow.

As you begin to get the hang of following the energy, opening and allowing, the next perfect step will come to you, and then the next, and the next and the next. You'll learn to open your human mind to the awareness that's always in and available to you that gives you the ability to perceive far beyond your limited physical senses.

Humans are closed off most of the time; you're largely perceiving yourselves and your realities through what you see, hear, taste, touch, smell, and think. And then you say, "This is what's real; this is what's logical; and this is how it is," which is so far from the truth of it. You limit Source energy, you limit divine orchestration, and you limit your power, because you're holding yourself in a lower level of consciousness where awareness is limited.

Open to infinite intelligence; divine will is always guiding you. It knows who you are, knows where you are, and knows the easiest, most effortless path to that which is in your highest and best good. Your human will never be able to figure this out, and most of the time, you can't even imagine or dream of what is possible for you.

This infinite intelligence is you; it's your higher self. And it has the grander perspective of this human experience and what is going on. It knows everything, everyone, and your best intersection points. It knows all in this tapestry of human existence, including what's possible for you. Open to that. Open to the knowing that there's something far greater going on here—beyond what you can perceive with your limited physical senses. And as you do, you will no longer try to figure it out with your limited human perspective. You will simply allow divine orchestration, true creation, magic, miracles, and incredible manifestations beyond anything that you can imagine for yourself in this moment.

We say time and time again: everything you wish to be, you already are. It is all within you and it always has been. And when you come into the truth of this, into your wholeness, your completeness, your worthiness, and really know that it's not about doing more or earning more or doing something else to be enough, you will be living at the highest levels.

When you come into that level of consciousness where you know your worthiness, you live in such a state of joy, peace, harmony, well-being, abundance, freedom, beauty, inspiration, and creativity that the next perfect step will come to you. Follow the energy, follow the light, and when it's not there, stop. You stop because being in your power in this moment and being conscious and present in this moment is where you can allow in the wholeness and completeness of all that you are. You can allow the Source energy, the God consciousness within you, and that is you, to flow through you and direct you to the next perfect step.

This is the energy that creates worlds, but it is also the energy that creates *your* world. And when you allow it, there is such a flow and such a perfect unfolding that all sorts of things come out of the blue—divine orchestration, synchronicities, and so much more. Every day is exciting and fun and magical and miraculous, and you realize that you already are everything you wish to be. That's when the real fun begins. That's when you can really open to the infinite potentials and possibilities.

Many teachers say that we need to do the inner work: we need to look inside, explore our beliefs, ask new questions, face our fears, and realign priorities. And then there are others that say just follow your heart, live in joy, and everything will sort itself out. Can you help us to reconcile these two perspectives?

It's a journey through different levels of consciousness, and there are different experiences and emotions at each level. When you're in the 3rd Dimension—the dimension of separation—you are experiencing separation from Source. Because of the density of this dimension, you experience far less of the total energy that is yours and available to you, which means you also harness less of that energy.

Because it is the dimension of separation, you're separate from what you want, and you're separate from what you need. You're separate from one another. Everything is out there. Lack and limitation is the primary experience in this dimension. And because you're not fully summoning all the Source energy that is available to you, you force things, you effort, and you try to push energy where you think it should go. It's the level of consciousness characterized by massive, determined action and "hard work."

Can you manifest things from this level of consciousness? Yes. But it takes much longer and a lot more effort. What's most important to recognize about this approach to manifestation is that you usually don't end up getting what you really wanted—the joy, the love, the harmony, the freedom, or the well-being. When you create from lack, limitation, fear, and not-enoughness, you only get more of the same. So, you might create the big house, the boat, and a huge bank account, but you will live in fear of losing it, because you created it from the 3D perspective.

When you begin to awaken, or have moments where you experience yourself beyond lack, limitation, and separation, you start questioning who you are and why you're here. As we said previously, a shocking event, such as a death, divorce, medical diagnosis, the loss of a business or a job, a bankruptcy, or some other unwanted experience can be the catalyst for awakening. It is a moment where a person can realize, "Hey, I'm still me, and I'm not those things that I was identifying with." So they begin to wonder, "Who am I and what's really going on here?"

If you have enough curiosity about these and similar questions, you begin to move yourself into the 4th Dimension of consciousness, which is the dimension of transformation. In this dimension, you recognize you can change yourself and your circumstances and conditions. You can heal your pain, work to better understand yourself, and change things about you and how you are living. This is the "inner work" of healing, fixing, changing, transmuting, and transforming.

You can say that the 3rd and 4th Dimensions are the ones where you "do the work." At least, they are where you have been taught and do indeed believe that you must work!

Many of you stay in the 4th Dimension for long periods of time—several years, perhaps decades or even lifetimes—but if you've drawn this information to you, you're ready to go to the next level. You're ready for the 5th Dimension of consciousness, which is the dimension of pure love and true or impeccable creation—manifestation without an agenda. At this level of consciousness within the journey, you realize you are Source energy, God consciousness, the Divine. Therefore, you are creating and re-creating from your fullness and wholeness, rather than lack and limitation. In this experience, manifestation is easy, effortless, and harmonious; what you want and need comes even before you know you need it, and there is an abundant supply of everything.

As we said earlier, "You get more of who you are, not what you want," which is why it's so important to be in your joy. There's no need to dip down into lower dimensions, into the experience of lack, limitation, fear, separation, struggle, and suffering, to expand and create. In fact, it's so much easier and more fun to expand and create from the higher dimensions.

In the 5th Dimension of consciousness, you recognize the pure love within yourself, within the other, and within all circumstances and conditions. It is the level of God consciousness, which is also known as unity consciousness or oneness consciousness. In this dimension, you realize that everything is Source energy—the energy that creates worlds—and you are automatically allowing more of it.

Your creations at this level come from divine will, which is aligned to the highest and best good for all. And, because they are from the Divine, they also tend to go beyond what you can imagine for yourself. Because you're drawing to you more and more of all that you are (and may not be aware of), you are in an experience of expanding awareness, expanding consciousness, which just brings more. Fifth Dimension is where you understand having fun makes you a magnet for more fun, and thereby more truth, enlightenment, and all good things.

The answer to your question about doing the work versus just having fun, is that everyone's correct. However, what any individual perceives they need "to do" is determined by their level of consciousness, by their beliefs.

If you are holding yourself in the 3rd Dimension, separate from Source, and you believe that creating in form is difficult, and that you must push and force and effort, then that is how it will be, until your awareness expands. The pathway to the 4th Dimension is the recognition that there is more to you and to life than you thought. If you move into the 4th Dimension of transformation—where you are constantly focused on transforming—yourself, others, and life circumstances—you will continue to draw to you more and more experiences that you perceive as needing fixing, healing, changing, or transforming. This is the nature of the 4th Dimension.

The pathway into the 5th Dimension of consciousness, the state of pure love, Heaven on Earth, a New Earth, is to go beyond the idea that anyone or anything needs to be fixed, changed, healed, or transformed. It is about going beyond judgment—of right or wrong, good or bad, worthy or unworthy, etc.—in every area of your life. As you shift your focus away from the mental activity of judging, and drop from your head into your heart, you can become aware of the aspect of you that is beyond your human and connected to All That Is; this is consciousness itself. The more you tune in to this aspect of yourself, the more space, the more peace, the more freedom you will feel. From this state of being, of presence, you will start to become aware of yourself as the powerful creator within your own creation. You will begin to see that it was your power all along—to focus, to choose, to give meaning. It really was you all along.

With this new level of awareness, you can powerfully choose to create your reality the way you wish it to be. By choosing love over fear, peace over war, freedom over bondage, joy over sorrow, and so on and so forth, you are elevating your consciousness, you are elevating your awareness, and you are elevating your perspective; you are not only seeing things from a grander perspective, but you are living from a grander perspective. You're elevating your consciousness and your rate of vibration, which means you are allowing more of the Source energy, the God consciousness that is you and that creates worlds to flow through you into physical form. This is the state of consciousness where you experience the miracles and the magic, the incredible manifestations, the magnificent out-of-the-blue ones. And they occur without force, effort, or struggle, and without you having to change or "work on" yourself.

Can you speak to the work that might be embraced within the 3rd and 4th Dimensions?

By "work" we simply mean choosing to be present and conscious in the moment.

Now, you could make being conscious and present in the moment a lot of work, or you could simply choose to be conscious and present in the moment.

For the realization of your own enlightenment, it comes down to choosing that nothing is worth leaving the present moment, your Heaven on Earth. It is the only place where you can truly experience joy and freedom and abundance and well-being and harmony and love.

When you find yourself wanting to argue with a person and tell them why they're wrong and why you're right, and why they should do it your way, and that they should change, stop and ask yourself, "Is this worth my Heaven on Earth? Is this worth my joy, my peace, my harmony, my love, my well-being?" Some might say, "Yes, it is, because that's the only way I'm going to get them to change." So, what you are saying is that you need to force another to see it and do it your way so that you can be happy. Yet, this is exactly how you get entangled in lower dimensions of consciousness.

Instead, you can choose a higher perspective, a higher level of consciousness by becoming present and conscious in the moment and choosing to align with the joy, the love, and the well-being that is already within you. Only then are you positively contributing to more joy, more love, more well-being for you, for the other, and for the world around you.

Let's say your focus is as simple as your loved one leaving breadcrumbs on the counter. You can choose that the breadcrumbs on the counter are worth your Heaven on Earth. In this, you would be having thoughts like, "This shouldn't be happening; I've asked them to clean these up before," and "They really don't care," and feeling resentment and frustration and annoyance. Or you could leave the breadcrumbs, or just wipe the counter and be happy and joyful and peaceful. It is your choice.

The breadcrumbs on the counter are neutral, but you're the one giving them meaning and, therefore, creating your experience of it. You can decide whether someone left them there to offend or disrespect you, or because "they are lazy or don't care," or you can choose a higher perspective.

As an example, you could think in that moment, "Wow, if this person wasn't here in physical form anymore, there'd be no breadcrumbs. What if they were gone tomorrow? Then these would be sacred breadcrumbs—little reminders of what they enjoyed while they were here in form." That perspective and awareness is available to you. What we want you to recognize is the perspective you are choosing is what's determining your level of consciousness and, therefore, creating your reality.

How do you choose joy, for example, when you meet someone–maybe in a potential business or personal relationship–and they disappoint you? As you simultaneously grapple with the disappointment and your advice to "just choose joy." If I'm to be responsible, I'll want to ensure I'm not taken advantage of. Would you please give us tips on how to feel joyous when dealing with challenging people who we may not particularly love?

If you can, embrace the perspective that whatever is going on is happening for you, not to you. Who knows, if that person hadn't disappointed you, you may have spent many years trying to create something with them, pushing and forcing energy to make it happen, and then never quite feel the desired sense of fulfillment in your creation.

So, anytime you notice that something is frustrating or disappointing, stop, come back into the moment, take three deep breaths, and then choose the perspective that whatever is happening is happening for you. Then let the energy and the light guide the way; let the next best step come to you. As you do this, you instantly open to new potentials and possibilities that could serve you in even greater ways, for the highest and best good of all. And because you're not in judgment, or pushing against, or creating resistance, there is a much greater opportunity for joy.

Most of you who are drawn to these teachings want to live very much what you would call normal lives. You have families. You have children. You have friends. You have businesses. You have work that you're doing in the world. And yet you wish to bring a higher level of consciousness and awareness into each of these aspects of your life.

Therefore, every time you notice that you're trying to push or force anything, stop, slow down, breathe, and come into the moment and choose the perspective that this is for you. Then ask, "What would bring me more joy?" or "How can I bring more play, more fun, more creativity to this?" In the asking, you'll probably instantly notice that you were unconsciously attempting to push and force energy somewhere it didn't want to go. You had moved yourself, unintentionally, into an experience of lower levels of consciousness because you imposed a belief of lack or limitation somewhere along the way. For example, you may have been thinking, "This is never going to be done on time," or "I don't have enough resources to get this done."

When you get really good at understanding that you don't want to create anything in that old energy anymore, and that you want all your creations to be based in love, harmony, peace, joy, well-being, freedom, abundance, and beauty, then you will make the choice to bring yourself into a level of consciousness that is in alignment with what you want, infusing that into all of your creations. In this state of being, you will notice that all things are done *through you*. Whereas in lower dimensions of consciousness, in lack and limitation and separation, you are constantly doing, doing, doing, and there is always more to be done.

Ultimately, your ability to create in higher levels of consciousness comes down to your thoughts about your own worthiness. If you know yourself as Source energy, as God consciousness, as Divine, as Light, and as the powerful creator within your own creation, connected to All That Is and to an infinite supply of resources that are always available to you and not separate from you, then you will create from that. If you know yourself as worthy of everything you want and need, and that it will show up even before you know you need it, then you will create from that. If you know you are a force field of consciousness and that the particles of infinite creation are always responding to you, then you will create from that. Elevate your consciousness into that level of knowing, then you'll be moving yourself into True Creation, where you will draw, attract, and magnetize a life beyond your wildest dreams. Then you are effortlessly allowing reality to move through you.

Know how worthy you are, instead of holding yourself separate from it and chasing after manifestations to prove your worthiness.

"The work" is easy once you understand what is happening. Be consciously aware when you're unconsciously holding yourself in lower dimensions—in lack, limitation, fear, separation, or judgment. Just notice it, take a breath, and come back into a level of consciousness where you can observe your human experiencing these things. But these things are not the truth of you; they are just thoughts, beliefs, and stories that you're telling yourself. Don't entangle with them. Instead, come back into presence, into consciousness, and choose an easy, effortless, harmonious path, aligned with the truth of you, which is joy, peace, love, beauty, harmony, freedom, well-being, and abundance.

PURPOSE AND AWAKENING

You've already spoken a little bit on purpose, but can you tell us, again if necessary, how to find and live our life purpose?

Our answer to this question is almost always the same. As we asked you earlier, what do you most want for the people that you love? What do you want to give them?

Happiness, peace, love.

Well, you cannot give what you do not have. As you embody that which you most want for the people and world you love, you are living your purpose. Embody happiness, embody peace, embody love; realize it and expand it within yourself, and you will be living your purpose.

You focused yourself into the human experience to be satiated in every moment by all that is here for you in form. You came into form to play, create, and do the things you love and that bring you joy. As you are doing these things, you're living your purpose. As you're tasting delicious foods, smelling beautiful fragrances, seeing gorgeous scenery, hearing enchanting music, and feeling the love, peace, joy, and harmony, you're living your purpose. And when you are full and filled up and allowing the Source energy that is you to flow through you, and be experienced by you, you are also living your purpose. Your purpose is to live fully, love fully, and be all that you are.

Be the infinite being of love and light that you are. That is your purpose.

You get distracted about life's purpose when you think, "I'm not living my purpose, because I haven't figured out what I'm supposed to be doing with my gifts and talents yet; I haven't started that business, gotten that relationship, made a specific amount of money, or helped enough people yet." Then you think you're failing at your purpose because you haven't accomplished a particular thing in the external world. The same goes for particular roles in life. Some people wonder if their purpose is to be a doctor, lawyer, healer, parent, teacher, or some other role.

None of what you accomplish in the external world is who you really are. So, when you're looking out there for your purpose and defining it as an external manifestation, you're always going to be holding yourself separate from it.

If you notice you are struggling with purpose, the first step is to come into the awareness of who you really are. Who are you? Feel the Source energy within you that is the truth of you—the joy, the peace, the love, the beauty, the harmony, the freedom, the well-being, the abundance. Then take that level of beingness with you, that level of consciousness, into everything you do and everywhere you go, and you will find the most enjoyable roles and activities that will manifest as byproducts of what you are doing.

If you think of your purpose as being a conduit for Source energy in the world, the more you open to Source energy and express who you are and allow it into your creations, the more you will be living your purpose. You call this shining your light.

When you are doubting or denying yourself, you are holding yourself apart from who you really are and from living your purpose here and now. "I'm not ready, I'm not good enough yet, I've got to make more money, I've got to work harder, I've to get more done, I've got to get my children to a certain level in their life, and then I'll be enough." This is why so many of you feel a sense of yearning for purpose while not knowing what that purpose is. You believe your purpose is what you do in the world rather than who you are. There is a very big difference.

What do you say to people who really want to make sure they figure out what it is they came here to learn? This question comes from the idea that we incarnate with specific lessons to learn, like patience or empathy or tapping into creativity. Perhaps each of us has some key lessons that, once learned, will deliver us freedom that we've heretofore not experienced.

One of the games that you play, and it's perfect, and there's no judgment from our side ever, is this idea that you're here to learn some lesson. It's another form of doubting and denying yourself. You say, "I'm not good enough yet because I'm not patient. I'm not good enough yet because I'm not empathetic. I'm not good enough yet because I'm not creative."

So you and many others set up these games and then play within them. Usually, you're very unconscious of the game you're playing, even though you've created the rules of the game.

It's really fun; then, when you come fully into realization—which is the integration of every part of you—and you find that you can re-create the rules of the game any way you want them to be. At this level of consciousness, you'll be playing a very different game, really having fun, and doing the things that you love and enjoy.

You are here for the expansion of your consciousness, but also for the expansion of consciousness. You are here to express all that you are, the Source energy that is you here in physical form, and you're here to choose the experiences you want to have.

As you continue to expand your awareness and consciousness, and as you begin to perceive in new ways and have a grander perspective of all that's going on here, you begin to see things differently. So, at one time it may have served your path to believe you're here to learn lessons; it may not serve you now. For some, the idea of learning lessons may have been the highest level of awareness they could realize based on their individual and the collective consciousness at the time. But we are excited to tell you that there is a lot more here for you to perceive that isn't part of your current reality that will be in the weeks, months, and years to come.

Brilliant. For the person nodding right now, perhaps wondering, "Where do I begin?" what would you tell them?

Our answer to that question would be another question, "What brings you joy?" And the person might say, "The people I love, my pets, being in nature, a beautiful sunrise or sunset, the birds, rainbows, beautiful music, candlelight, a hug, a warm bath, swimming, gardening, walking outside," or whatever it is.

You're automatically beginning, now more than ever, to become aware of those things that bring you joy. And we would say, "Do that. Focus on those things." Some people would even be more specific—"I love to have deep, meaningful conversations about spirituality," or

"I love to read books about this." "I love creating things like that," whether it's music or poetry or painting, or "I love helping others."

Anything that you love can bring you into greater levels of awakening, greater levels of realization. But, again, your thoughts about your worthiness are critical. If you're doing the things you love, but then thinking you should, have to, or are supposed to be doing something else, something more "responsible," or you believe that you could get it wrong, could fail, are not enough, then you are playing in the illusion of unworthiness. This is a game the human plays to hold themself in limitation.

When you know that you are worthy and have always been, you will do the things that bring you joy. You will play and create, fully living your purpose along the way, contributing to the elevation of consciousness and the raising of vibration by doing what you love. It's important to see, however, that someone would only ask this question if they do not believe in their inherent worthiness. In this case, they believe they should do, need to do something to be enough. Then and only then will they be worthy of being happy and joyful.

What are you supposed to do? Do the things that bring you joy. Sleep, rest, read a book, go for a walk, talk to your favorite person, have a cup of tea, eat a beautiful meal, grow a garden, smell the flowers, sit in the grass, and feel the sunshine on your face, whatever it is. In doing what you love and what is joyful, you will self-realize. Inspiration, creativity, enthusiasm will all be realized by you in those states of doing what's joyful and what you love.

I would think if somebody said, "But I shouldn't," or "But this," then that is what they came to learn. So, do they just ignore that voice in their head, follow their heart, and do what they love despite those thoughts?

The voice in the head that says, "I can't" or "I shouldn't" isn't what they came to learn. That message is just a belief system they picked up along the way. It's a way they hold themself in lack and imitation because they don't think they are worthy yet.

When you entertain those kinds of thoughts, your human isn't taking full responsibility for being the powerful creator that you are. Like when you say, "Well, he won't let me, or she won't let me, or they won't let me, or I have too many things to do, and I have all these things I'm responsible for, and I must do all these other things first, and only then will I be worthy." In this moment, you have the power to create anything you choose for you, and you can do so in a loving, harmonious way. We understand there can be fear and discomfort in taking full responsibility for yourself as creator within your own creation, but true freedom and true creation is not possible without it.

When someone wants to or has tried to make changes in their life but doesn't have the level of awareness or consciousness that they can do it in a loving, harmonious way, they will push and force and effort and attempt to get others to do what they want them to do to get the change that they want to experience. Others get triggered and react, and then the person wanting the change says, "Oh, it's just not worth it. I'll just stay stuck because it's too difficult to try to navigate through to what I want to create." In lower dimensions of consciousness, change can seem incredibly frustrating, and resistance is common.

Navigating through change (which we prefer to call navigating through creation) from higher levels of consciousness is much easier. As you come into alignment to the truth of who you are and the power within you, you will begin to see that there is only love, which is the most transformative energy on the planet. And as you embody the love that you are and see all others as love, you will navigate through creation from the highest levels of consciousness, aligned to that pure love. Then anything and everything can come into form in the most easy, effortless, harmonious, amazing ways.

Most of you haven't experienced creation from this level of consciousness. When you do, you will realize that anything and everything is possible for you. And from that perspective you will see why it was difficult in the past and why navigating through creation is much easier and more harmonious from the state of pure love.

ISSUES OF OUR WORLD TODAY

Thank you. Humanity is going through a lot right now as a species—a global pandemic, polarization, another war. In some ways, it seems to be independent of us, though I know that's not the case. Can you give us a historical perspective?

Everything that's happening on the planet at this time can be seen from the grander perspective that this is bringing all things back into an alignment with the truth of the Source energy and the pure love within everything.

It may seem like things are going wrong, falling apart, or however else you describe it. But if you reflect on different times in your life, when you felt the same way about shifting circumstances, you will see that some of those experiences were extraordinary catalysts for your awakening and realization. If you reflect on who you've become and where you are now, in terms of your level of consciousness and awareness, you will see that many of those experiences have led to more love, more joy, and more of everything you've ever wished for in your life.

And rest assured the same is true for all of humankind. In fact, even when you can't see the benefits of a shift, you can rest assured they exist. Again, everything happens for you.

For the transformational times you're living in, now when you choose the illusions of separation, it's going to feel more awful to you than ever before. This creates an opportunity for you to be consciously aware of whether you're choosing pure love and the truth that Source is within everything. Otherwise, you're contributing to the suffering.

When you choose love, you will know that everything's happening for you, that everything is always working out for you. You will see everything from a grander perspective. You will come into an awareness—as creator within your own creation—that everything is perfect. Your reality is always a perfect reflection of the level of consciousness from which you have been creating. And when you take full responsibility for this, you will no longer blame anyone or anything outside of you.

I'd like to understand our transformation today versus other times when perhaps there was as much or more enlightenment, like with the civilizations of Atlantis and Lemuria. Is this the greatest transformation of human consciousness in history because it eclipses the highest highs of earlier civilizations or because it's more global in nature?

Well, you have far more people in your human collective today than ever before. From that perspective the transformation is greater. It is also greater, however, because of what is shifting; you are transcending the illusion of separation, even more so than in other civilizations where beings may be existing at higher levels of consciousness and awareness. Understand that from higher levels of consciousness—5th Dimension and above—there is just an expansion of the light and the love that you are.

From our perspective, this really is the greatest thing happening in all the universe. You chose to focus yourself into this experience at this time; isn't this proof that it's the greatest thing going on right now in all the universe? You chose it. If there was something better going on somewhere else, don't you think you'd be there?

Is it possible that I'm there too?

Indeed! You are a multidimensional being, and there are aspects of you having all kinds of experiences in different levels of consciousness throughout eternity and beyond. These aspects are not separate from you but are in levels of consciousness that you cannot perceive while in this physical experience.

When you can accept that your human mind will never fully understand all of what is going on here, you can begin to focus your attention on feeling it. You can feel your way into unity consciousness and into the oneness. As you feel your way into that, you will be able to feel yourself as the center of your universe, you will be able to feel yourself into the Isness of All That Is, and you will be able to feel yourself as creator within your own creation. You will literally begin to perceive yourself into realities where you can feel the entire universe within you. There's no separation from anything ever.

In time, you will elevate your consciousness to even greater awareness of what lies beyond. But for those of you who have drawn this information to you, your journey is now about coming into realization and living as the embodied masters you are, helping to raise the collective vibration on this planet at this time. You excitedly chose to be here and to realize and to create the greatest possible life that you can imagine.

The realization of who you are as Source energy will be embodied in the human experience at this time. That is why you're here and that is why you are so very important. And as we've said, there is a far greater purpose for Earth in this vast and glorious universe as you individually and collectively elevate your vibrational frequencies and consciousness.

I'd like to broaden the conversation to what the world is going through, particularly with extreme polarization in politics—although you could just call it views on life and reality. Is this polarization as simple as seeing those who have chosen fear versus those who have chosen love? Am I overly simplifying it? Why the extreme polarities, where people seem to disagree so vehemently, when previously there appeared to be more tolerance and compromise?

This might surprise you, but from our perspective, there is more peace, more harmony, more collaboration, and more cooperation on your planet than ever before. And there are more people who are seeking to come together to collaborate new changes and co-create than ever before.

That's our perspective. Truly, there is more love. More people are living in joy, peace, harmony, well-being, and abundance than ever before, and more people are experiencing freedom than ever before.

What you focus on and the meaning you're giving it is creating your reality. There may have been greater wars on your planet in previous times, but less or no media coverage and fewer social platforms greatly diminished people's "experience" of these wars.

The key is to focus yourself into a grander perspective of what's really going on here. What you are witnessing is simply a perception within a dimension of consciousness based on separation. You can elevate yourself beyond right-doing and wrongdoing at any point in time. And the more of you who do that, the less the collective will focus upon it. Soon enough, you will find those observations aren't part of your reality anymore.

Taking this a step further, as you seek to collaborate, cooperate, and co-create new structures and systems founded in more peace, harmony, abundance, joy, well-being, and freedom, you will find it's far easier when you're not trying to push and force change upon the old.

You are never going to come to a resolution through fighting or warring. Just like you will never come to a resolution by trying to figure out or account for who is right or wrong, or how many times they were right or wrong. In that level of consciousness, you will only be holding yourself and others in an experience of separation.

More of you than ever before, in this human experience, are elevating yourself beyond these lower levels of consciousness. And as you continue, you will realize more peace, more harmony, more joy, more collaboration, and more cooperation in your experience until it becomes your way of being in the world, your continuous experience of reality.

You have the power within you to observe anything in the human experience while staying in a state of pure love and not entangling with the illusion of separation. You could sit and watch a heated political argument, for example, and recognize the pure love within, all while enjoying the passion, personalities, and flow of energy, without entangling in the content. And if you really held your presence, focused in such a high vibration of oneness, realization, and unity consciousness, allowing the Source energy that you are to flow through you, you cannot even imagine the spontaneous realizations and awakenings you'd experience.

When you're entangled in the right-doing and wrong-doing, you are actively moving that energy through you, through your body and beyond.

We recognize there are many challenges for the human in lower dimensions of consciousness, yet we still very much advocate that you live fully in this world. Again, you do not need to live on a mountaintop as a monk unless that is your choosing. Most of you who are drawn to this very much want to be involved in the world and all the experiences now unfolding.

You have the power within you and the Source energy available to you to show up fully present in every area of your life. You're not going to do this to try to change anyone or any circumstance or situation; you're going to do it because of how good it feels to live in your truth. You will then see the power of True Creation with no agenda, and you'll witness magic, miracles, and manifestations on levels you've never experienced before. This is what is possible for all of you.

Looking beyond the COVID-19 pandemic, what is behind *any* illness? A cold or allergies, hay fever, cancer, heart disease, arthritis–all of it? Is it genes, beliefs, emotions, disconnection, stress, confusion? Is there an answer you could give us that would cover all these health concerns?

Let us begin answering this question by giving you the highest vision for health and well-being. We'll also give you the potentials and possibilities for health and well-being inside of different levels of consciousness.

First, what is possible for each of you is to live at such a high level of well-being that the cells in your body regenerate and rejuvenate at expeditious rates, and you continue to create and re-create the highest level of health and well-being. By fully allowing Source energy to flow through you, you allow the cells and the body to operate at their highest levels.

While it is completely possible now for humanity to elevate its consciousness such that you all live at much higher levels of vibration and frequency, it is more difficult now because of the beliefs in your collective around disease. Sickness, pain, and lack of health do not exist in higher dimensions; they are only manifestations in lower levels of consciousness.

Still, all disease is happening for you. Yet from your perspective you almost always perceive it as wrong or as something that shouldn't be happening. Some of the greatest awakening experiences on your planet have occurred in people who experienced disease or disharmony in the body, and because of it they remembered who they really are. They remembered that they are not their body, and so they chose to perceive themselves beyond it. In that moment, releasing all resistance, the body was also able to transcend the limitation and come back into wholeness.

In realization, there is always an expansion of consciousness. As your consciousness expands, so does what you believe is possible for you. Then what you experience as possible and how you create your reality begins to expand as well.

In the 3rd Dimension of consciousness, you and most others would say that you are your body. You believe yourselves to be a personality and the human you know yourself to be. You think you are this body, and you're perceiving reality through it. In this dimension, people say, "This is who I am, this is all there is, and there is nothing I can do about it." You begin to relate to your body as tall enough or not tall enough, too thin or too heavy, too old or too young, and on and on. In this dimension of consciousness, there is a continuous focus on what's wrong with your body.

You also have many emotions that hold you in heavy, dense levels of consciousness, which lowers your rate of vibration and frequency. Because you're not fully allowing Source energy through you in these states, there is a lack, slowing, or imbalance in the flow of energy, which causes disruptions and misalignments. These occur first in the energetic layer and then in the emotional layer and eventually in the physical layer, where disease becomes manifest.

We would never say that anyone would ever intentionally, consciously choose to manifest disease, disharmony, pain, lack, or limitation in the body. We do not say, "Oh, you caused your own sickness or disease." However, as you come into higher levels of awareness, you become more empowered, more intentional in your creations, and you can perceive a reality where health and well-being are always available to you, no matter what you are experiencing in this moment.

Many people who have experienced severe disease, pain, or sickness in the body, or had near-death experiences related to illnesses, began to ask questions: "Who am I?" "Who am I beyond this body that is struggling so much?" In those moments, you are beginning to perceive yourself into higher levels of consciousness and realizing that there is something within you that goes beyond the physical body. That is you beginning to perceive yourself into the 4th Dimension of consciousness, where you become aware that you can transform your body. Many great masters have shared with humankind the correlation between disharmony in the energetic and emotional layers that manifests as disharmony in the physical layer. They teach and have even demonstrated that as you clear, heal, repair, and transform the energetic and emotional layers, the physical body can do the same.

While we see, and agree, that you oftentimes get very stuck and spend many years in this dimension of transformation—always trying to heal, always trying to fix, always trying to release, always working on yourself, always searching for more ways to restore harmony to your body—it is part of the journey through different levels of consciousness. Yet at this level, where you are continuously perceiving you and your body as something to fix, you will unknowingly continue to draw to you things that are wrong or perceived as wrong in the body that need to be changed, healed, and transformed.

To move into higher levels of consciousness, go beyond your judgment of what has manifested in the body. Rather than thinking of it as right or wrong, or needing to be fixed, choose to know that everything is always happening for you. In this you are not rejecting what is. Then see if you can embrace it and open to receive the gifts, the miracles, the expansion that occurs as you begin creating in higher levels of health and well-being in the physical body.

What happens with so many of you when you have symptoms is that you start to push against it and create resistance: you react to it and try to fix it or fight it. And you're thinking, "What's wrong with me?" So, in your reaction, you are lowering your level of consciousness and then trying to change it from there, which will just result in more fixing and fighting.

Yet another possibility when you notice symptoms is to go within, right here right now, and focus your attention on creating the highest well-being within you in the moment. Align every cell of your body to come into balance, into harmony, and into joy.

And if you continue to do this—to slow down, go within, and create well-being within you—instead of trying to push and force and effort your way through the disharmony, you will move your body into a state of well-being much more easily, effortlessly, and harmoniously. Once you come into the realization of the state that you want to experience, such as balance, harmony, and joy, then you may have an awareness of exactly what is out of alignment in the emotional or physical layers. But you will be doing this from a much higher perspective, aligned with your highest well-being.

Anyone who has ever had a spontaneous healing experience came to a point where they just fully and completely let go of their resistance. They let go of the pain, they let go of pushing and the forcing, and they let go of the fear of the disease, the fear of the pain, and in some cases, the fear of dying. For one moment, they went completely beyond all the resistance into total surrender, into total allowing; they just let go of it all. That is when the Source energy could begin to move through them in such a way that it restored wholeness to their body. You do not have to wait until you have a full-blown, life-threatening disease to practice aligning with your highest well-being. You can consciously and intentionally flow Source energy into every cell in your body, in any moment.

Many ask me, why doesn't Source energy or God get rid of all the suffering and evil in the world? I have my own answers for this that bring me total peace, but it's one of those universal questions that many on this path hear. Would you give us your perspective?

There are a couple of things here. First, all of you are in an experience of free will, which means that nothing outside of you can choose for you. If you choose to believe that you're not good enough, not loved, not worthy, a victim of life circumstances, and that terrible things happen to you, that nothing ever works out for you, and that life is not fair, then you will hold yourself in a level of consciousness and density of vibration where you indeed experience suffering. Thus, you have the free will to choose your own suffering as much as you have the free will to choose your own joy. It all comes down to the thoughts that you're thinking and the meaning that you are giving things, which affects the level of consciousness that you are in at the time.

The root of all suffering is the belief that you are unworthy, not good enough, and unloved by Source, by God, by Creator—the very thing that you are. As we said earlier, you must work very hard to hold yourself in lower vibrations of consciousness; it takes a lot of energy to deny the truth of you and your magnificence.

Individuals and collectives within humanity forget the truth of who they are; they forget their magnificence. In this, they are perceiving reality from the lower levels of consciousness where the unworthiness, the unlovableness, and the not-good-enoughness exist and create great suffering for themselves and others. You are all Source, God, the Divine. God is in you, God is in everyone, and God is in everything, and you are either focused on perceiving the God within you and others and everything, and the love within you and others and everything, or you are choosing to perceive the lack of Source, of God, of love in you and others and everything. It is always your choice.

Many times, in your human experience, you encounter upsetting situations. In the moment, you create a story about it as being the most awful thing that could ever happen. You say things like: "It's terrible. It's horrible. It's wrong. It shouldn't have happened. Why me? God doesn't love me. I must be unlovable." And you're angry, mad, and filled with rage. You are suffering and struggling. Yet, you may continue to create your suffering by repeating the story over and over again while feeling the emotions of it. You may even drag your friends and family into the suffering with you and find others that have had similar experiences who are suffering too; then there's a group of you suffering together. This is how you perpetuate suffering in lower dimensions of consciousness.

However, in the journey through different levels of consciousness, maybe you're fortunate enough to have an experience that allows you to see a higher perspective. Let's say the upsetting situation is a breakup, the end of a relationship, and you are so hurt, so angry, so mad, and feeling vindictive; they've wronged you, they've abused you, and they are a terrible person, and this is the worst thing that's ever happened to you. So, in your suffering you pray to God to fix it and make it better. Then, a few months or years later, you meet an incredible person who's the love of your life. You are so happy and can hardly believe that you've come together with this person to create such a beautiful, harmonious, loving relationship. Now, when you look back at that breakup, you might say, "Oh, that was the best thing that ever happened to me." Suddenly, God is good and "on your side" because of all the good things now happening in your life.

When you create and re-create the story that life is difficult and a struggle, and it's bad, and bad things are happening, and there are bad people out there, and you continue to focus upon it, you are creating more suffering for yourself and more suffering in the world.

Many of you ask us about the suffering of others. Our response is always the same: you will always cause your own suffering when you think you know what another soul's journey should be. You do not know why another person is going through what they're going through, but you can either suffer along with them—thereby contributing to their suffering, your suffering, and the suffering in the world—or you can go into a higher level of consciousness and remember the truth—of them, of you, and of everything: everything is always happening for all of you, Source energy is within you and in all things and always available to you, and you can create your world in any way you wish it to be. It is always your choice. And as you can choose to remember the truth of the other, and know that, in their time and in their way, they will remember the truth of who they are too, you will be able to allow them to be where they are. You will not push or force or effort, and you will not try to impose your free will on them or choose for them because you do not agree with where they are on their path.

When you are trying to choose for another and thinking they are on the "wrong path" and it's not where they should be, you are believing in and participating in the illusions of lack, limitation, and separation.

Now, and this is important: none of this is to suggest you not be of assistance to others in pain, not to lend a hand, or not to get involved if this is your soul's urging. Nor are our words meant to excuse violent or hurtful behavior. We are here to offer you a grander perspective of all circumstances and to remind you that there is no reason to deny your worthiness or deny love for yourself for any reason.

All of you are on journeys through different levels of consciousness. Yet you want to tell someone where they should be or where they should go; you want to choose for them, even when most of the time you don't like it when others do this to you. We use the example most of you can relate to of different foods in childhood. If you think back to when you were younger, you had a certain palette of flavors. There were things you really loved to eat, things you didn't necessarily want to eat that your parents made you eat, and things that you thought were disgusting. Now, as an adult, most of you don't eat the same things you ate as a child. In fact, many of you now eat the disgusting things you never thought you would ever eat!

Your preferences change on your journey, and so does how you see and experience things. You have experiences that bring you into new levels of awareness, and your consciousness expands as a result. *Your responsibility is to your path.* So, if there is suffering in your world, then go within and create the world within you that you want to experience in the world around you. And as you do this, others will remember that they, too, have the power to create a world of joy, peace, freedom, love, harmony, abundance, and well-being whenever it is of their choosing.

Is it God causing the suffering in the world? No. It's the belief in the separation from God—from the God within you, the God within all others, and the God within everything—that is creating the suffering.

You will also experience suffering when you forget that nothing is ever destroyed; it only ever changes form. There is no end to creation, ever. When you think that creation has ended, you are, again, believing in the illusion. If a tidal wave or a volcano devastates a town and you think it's gone, you'll suffer in that illusion. Yet, if you can observe it from a higher perspective, you will often see that what is born out of the destruction is more love, kindness, compassion, inspiration, creativity, and innovation. It's all perception, and it is all of your choosing.

Each of you has the power to fully allow Source energy to guide you through your life in a way where you would never entangle with any circumstances or conditions that weren't of your highest and best good. For example, you could be walking down a path thinking you should turn right, until something suddenly guides you to keep going straight. This is how Source energy works. You follow the energy, letting this inner light guide your way because you are present and conscious, opening and allowing. Happy and unquestioning, you might never know that in listening to that guidance you were avoiding some catastrophe occurring on the other path.

You will experience life in a very different way as you fully open to the Source energy within you. You will find yourself living in such a flow, letting energy and light guide the way, and observing the events of the world from a grander perspective; and you won't go into reaction, resistance, or entanglement.

If we were to ask you what the world needs most from you now, not one of you would say "contributing to the suffering and the struggle and the lack and the limitation and the fear and the separation." Nor would any of you say, "Well, I think the best thing that I can do for the world is to suffer enough myself so that everybody around me can become more joyful."

The greatest contribution you can make is to elevate your consciousness and your vibration into joy, peace, love, abundance, harmony, freedom, well-being, and beauty. In every moment that you choose this, through your own free will, you are choosing to be in your power, fully allowing Source energy to flow through you, showing the way for others to see what is possible for them too.

With anything in life, you can always tell the level of consciousness with which you are relating to by the way that you feel. You will always know how closely you are aligned to your truth by how you feel.

As we said before, some will argue for their limitations. They will say, "It really is awful; these *are* terrible things, and it's inexcusable that these people are suffering." But you will not be seeing all there is to see. This is fighting for your limitations. It will simultaneously be true that everyone is a divinely powerful being of infinite light and love. And in time, in their own way, because it is their journey, they, too, will awaken and remember the power within them.

From our perspective, we only and always see the truth of you, the complete picture. We see and know the power within you. We can see you no other way. And as you begin to see yourself and others this way, you will witness an extraordinary transformation, not only in yourself but also in others and the world as well. And we remind you, you're not going to do this because you're trying to change anyone or anything; you're doing it because in seeing the truth, of yourself, others, and everything, you live your highest purpose and expression, which leads to your greatest expansion.

ENLIGHTENMENT AND PERSONAL AWAKENING

Earlier I asked what life might look like if I was living in a higher dimension. You beautifully described what a perfect day would look like, including the joy and excitement that would be present in an enlightened experience. To expand on that, what might the world, planet Earth, look like in, say, 100 years, when humanity has reached a higher level of consciousness? Beyond individuals moving through their days with joy, what might the world look like in the realms of communications,

learning, entertainment, business, political structure, work, community, and currency– the fundamentals? How will the dream of life play out? Do you have a bird's-eye view to offer us?

First, understand that the world you see around you is a reflection of the world that exists within you. If you are living in the struggle and suffering, if you are believing in limited resources, if you are angry, resentful, and at war within yourself, and if you are in chaos and fear and judgment within, that is the world you will experience around you.

The reason for our wisdom is so you can remember that what you create within you, you create in the world around you. As you create a world within you that is peaceful, joyful, harmonious, loving, kind, abundant, and full of beauty, well-being, and freedom, you are creating this in the world around you. So many of you are doing this now; you are bringing yourself into oneness, into unity consciousness, into God consciousness. And in doing it for yourself, you are doing it for humanity. You are helping to elevate the consciousness of humanity into a state of oneness. And you're not doing it so all of you will choose the same things and the same ways of living. You're doing it so that you all operate at a level of consciousness aligned to your truth. And it will never matter who's not choosing that which you choose for yourself; you will simply go deeper into creating the world within you that you want to experience in the world around you.

There is an incredible transformation of consciousness happening on the planet at this time. Individually and collectively, you are stepping into levels of consciousness, vibration, and frequency that are incredibly exciting. You are going to see the greatest innovations and the greatest technological advancements that you've ever seen. You're going to see a complete upleveling of humankind.

That's what is possible. However, it is always of your choosing; so it comes down to you living your version of Heaven on Earth. Realize that you are on this planet, moving through the universe, as one collective human family, but you are unique within yourself—with endless potentials and possibilities to expand, explore, express, and choose the experiences that you would like to have. Each of you can tap into inspiration from infinite intelligence and use it to innovate and to expand technologies and systems and all kinds of things. As you go beyond the illusions of lack and limitation and separation, humanity will too; and there is no end to the expansion that is possible.

You have enough resources on this planet to completely satiate your entire human family; in fact, there is an infinite supply of available resources for all of you now. As you shift your focus and attention away from warring, chaos, and division, and stop trying to change people and situations, and stop arguing about who's right and wrong, you will be elevating your consciousness into a place of inspiration that allows you to perceive optimal potentials for resource-sharing and exchange systems based in understanding one's own worth and one's own value.

Those who are awakening within organizations, corporations, businesses, and as entrepreneurs will lead in ways that are aligned to their truth—following the energy and light, being and staying in the flow, and allowing Source energy and the inspiration and creativity that comes with it.

The future for humankind can be as beautiful and glorious as you can imagine it. Your path to that is to create it within yourself while holding the vision for a fully awakened world where all beings live in harmony with one another—all humans and all animals and the entire planet *living as one*. And in this, there is peace, joy, love, abundance, harmony, freedom, and well-being for all.

Keep in mind that you can only choose for yourself; you don't get to choose for others. But as you continue to elevate your own consciousness and vibration, you positively contribute to elevating it for all on planet Earth. And when consciousness reaches a certain vibrational frequency, many will spontaneously awaken to their truth. And you will notice a very rapid expansion of consciousness where people begin to move into transformation and then into pure love.

In lower levels of consciousness, you think there are all these problems that need to be fixed, all these things that need to be changed, and all these systems and structures that need to be rebuilt. Then we come along and say to you, "It's all about consciousness." Well, if you investigate this in your own life, you will begin to understand that all the solutions and answers you seek are already here; they are just in an elevated level of consciousness. The highest guidance, the most expansive awareness, and the grander perspectives of what is possible—all of it is here.

The answer to everything, including the answer to creating the future you want for humankind is consciousness, and it starts with your own. The more you elevate your consciousness, the more you are positively contributing to and elevating the consciousness of humanity. You will reach a place where you will experience a natural gravitation to oneness, unity, and a desire for love, peace, joy, harmony, abundance, freedom, and well-being for all.

It is very easy to understand how all this occurs when you understand the different levels of consciousness. When you're perceiving yourself in separation—right and wrong, lack and limitation, and fear—you're in a very dense vibration or frequency. As each of you continue to move into higher levels of consciousness, it just gets easier for you and much easier for all those who are also finding their way.

We often refer to you as wayshowers, and you are, indeed, forging new paths, blazing new trails, and going beyond what you ever thought possible. So let's say you were out hiking in nature, and you could see the mountaintop from where you were, but the path that you were traveling on—the one that most people took—meandered this way and that way around the mountain and would take a very long time to get to the top. But you saw a quicker, easier, more effortless path. So you began moving through the trees and the brush, thereby paving a new path, a new way, to the top. And if you continued to take that new path every time you hiked to that mountaintop, then more people would start taking that path. Suddenly this quicker, easier, more effortless path would be taken by all.

We have another analogy. For generations, the way you and your family got from one side of the river to the other was to wade across. You got wet each time, but sometimes you got really wet because you were washed down the river in the currents. But that was the only way across the river, and you needed to get across—for food, for supplies, for work—so you did it. Each time, you might be wet, cold, and exhausted, but you got to the other side of the river. If suddenly one day you went to the river and there was a bridge there, and you saw people walking across the bridge, you would just take the quicker, easier, more effortless way across the water.

So all you've got to do for yourself and humankind is to build a bridge into higher levels of consciousness. You do this by living at a higher level of consciousness; you choose higher-level thoughts that create higher-level emotions that increase your vibration and frequency and expand your potentials and possibilities. And as you build your bridge, you are making it so much easier for all of humankind to build theirs.

I've heard from some authors and spiritual teachers that a time may come very soon where a gigantic wave of energy moves through the physical universe, bringing with it spontaneous enlightenment for many. Is there something to that? If so, then how much of an upliftment can we expect? Will someone who's well into this work, studying it, loving it, enjoying it be automatically bumped to an ascended level, or will everybody just feel a little bit lighter, if anything?

The potential and the possibility of that kind of wave of enlightenment absolutely exists. But we don't want you to create an experience of separation, as if you're waiting for it, as if something outside of you is going to make it happen for you.

Continue to perceive it. Continue to focus upon it. Continue to give it such meaning that you are moving it into reality. It's not a passive state; you aren't waiting for the cosmic enlightenment to occur. You are consciously, proactively, intentionally creating that reality by focusing your attention on it, which brings it into physical form.

As we've said, consciousness moves energy into form. You're talking about a big, massive wave of enlightenment energy, and your consciousness of it is what moves it into form.

May a time come when all of humankind is choosing to remember who they are? Absolutely. And as you witness the magic of it in you and in others around you, and celebrate it, and focus upon it, and create it, you expand the possibility of it.

You matter and your life matters, and you choosing your highest realization, which is to come into and live as the embodied master that you are, really matters. Every single one of you reading this can come into realization. You can choose it now.

However, your human is never going to figure out how to do it. Your human can only allow it. Your human can allow the spontaneous cosmic enlightenment energy, or your human can deny it. Don't try to figure it out or intellectualize it; just get yourself into a place where your human allows it. As much as you can, come into the present moment and allow the Source energy that is you and is within you to flow through you; that is allowing.

Of course, anything's possible, but some things have a greater probability than others. So, I'm curious. What is the probability right now for the manifestation of all the good things–awakening, realization, love, joy, peace, abundance?

Well, the probability is 100 percent. It's true. Now, how many of you will experience all of this as a 100 percent probability in this lifetime? Well, that's of each person's choosing. You'll either realize in this human incarnation, or you will realize when you release the density of the body and reemerge into higher levels of consciousness. You'll get there either way, guaranteed.

This is a grand adventure, but it is also a journey through levels of consciousness. Are there laws of the universe such that some things work perfectly no matter what? Yes.

As you come into the experience of being fully enlightened, you're going to realize you can bring forth the light that you are into everything. In that state of being, you won't limit yourself to only doing certain things. And you will continue to realize abundance and harmony as you journey into higher levels of consciousness.

When you're in lower levels of consciousness, it takes a lot of energy to plan and to strategize and to organize all the details; then, once you have the plan, you usually start pushing and forcing and efforting to make those things happen. It's a lot of work. As you move into higher levels of consciousness and allow more light, you will be in a higher vibration and frequency, and a whole lot more Source energy will be flowing through you. In these levels, creation is so much easier, so much more fun, and so much more effortless and harmonious. And because there is so much more Source energy in all of that, the energy you receive from those creations will be on levels you've never experienced before. There will be much more abundance, much more prosperity, and an even deeper, richer, more expansive experience of life.

The greatest wealth on your planet now—and in times to come—is consciousness. Getting into a vibrational frequency where you're fully allowing Source energy through you will make you the wealthiest person on the planet. And by wealth, we not only mean money, but an infinite supply of everything you need and more—resources, connections, opportunities, time, love, creativity, and inspiration.

All of this is available to you now if it is your choosing. And you will continue to create what you're inspired to create, when you're inspired to create it, giving and receiving fully from your place of wholeness, knowing that the energy of giving and receiving is one. You have been trained for so long to think that if you want to receive, you've got to give—more and more and more. So many of you are just giving and giving and giving, yet you never open up to receive; you don't allow yourself to receive. So, open yourself up to receiving; there is a vast amount of wealth, abundance, prosperity, and resources here for you when you start allowing yourself to receive.

If giving and receiving are out of balance, you will know it. You will be pushing and forcing; you will hear that voice inside that says, "You've got to do more. You've got to give more." But if you would just spend all that time you had planned to do more, to fully allow yourself to receive, we assure you the abundance will be beyond anything you could imagine.

What are the steps to allowing myself to receive? How do we do it? The first thing I think of is to hold out my hands, but that seems passive.

Well, it doesn't have to be. You are creator within your own creation, so you could sit comfortably in a chair and open your hands to receive. Then you could powerfully focus, in your mind, a holographic image of you receiving beautiful light from every direction. The brightest, most magnificent golden light of abundance, prosperity, and well-being; this incredible light contains everything you could ever desire and more, and it is flowing into you from every direction through your open hands. And at some point, you are so focused on the brilliance and energy of the light that you cannot tell whether the energy is coming from your hands or flowing into your hands. You are so fully allowing the light to flow through you, and so powerfully experiencing it as your reality, that it is projected into the world around you. That is allowing yourself into the energy of receiving.

Remember: You are Source. You are God. You are Creator. You are the Divine. You are the Source energy that you move into form as you focus your consciousness. All the energy is here for you; it's all your energy. Consciousness moves energy into form. When you are visualizing receiving, you are consciously projecting a holographic image of you powerfully receiving into your reality; every cell in your body is responding to that as if it is your reality in the here and now. You live in a far more holographic reality than you realize. So as you begin to focus your consciousness, energy begins responding to you, and you begin to move all kinds of experiences into physical form in easy, effortless, harmonious, and miraculous ways.

All the energy is here for you, which means everything is here for you. Nature, the land, the air, the sunlight, the stars, the sun, the moon, the waves in the ocean, the grass beneath your feet, the animals, the birds, the butterflies, the mountains, the rivers, the streams, the rain, and the wind—it's all here for you. Everything is here for you. Every opportunity, every resource, every connection you could ever need, and all the money, time, space, support, and love. It's all here for you. So, as you come into the realization of this, and begin to experience True Creation, you will move yourself fully into the knowing of you as the powerful creator of your reality. And you will begin to create in a whole new world that you've never perceived yourself into before while in physical form. In this world, you get more of what you are, what you're focused upon, and what you're projecting into your field of consciousness. And you choose the experiences you want to have for you.

At some point, your creation of reality will only happen from this level of consciousness; never again will you need to "work" so hard for what you want. You will be consciously expressing Source energy through you, and you will be choosing the experiences that you want to have, in this magnificent experience that is all here for you.

Thank you, Council.

CONNECTING WITH OUR ANGELS AND SPIRIT GUIDES

As we near the end of this section, The Journey, I think many people in the throes of this grand experience in time and space would be happy to hear how to get in touch with their angels and spirit guides and how to work with them. You told us earlier that these connections exist; how do we make contact?

Each of you has already made contact. You may not yet have conscious awareness that your human is the one doing this work, but it is. As your human asks for an experience of higher levels of awareness, it knows that somewhere within you it's available—in the higher realms.

We've spoken about the dimensions of consciousness. In the 3rd Dimension, which is a dimension of density in this plane of demonstration that you call Earth, you experience physical form. This is not a bad thing. Everything is of Source. However, in this denser and heavier reality, vibrations and frequencies are slower. As such, there are different things and experiences available in this level of consciousness. As you elevate your consciousness and allow in more levels of light and Source energy, there are more experiences available to you.

Indeed, all sorts of different beings focus themselves into these higher dimensions of consciousness for the experiences that exist within them.

What you call angels, archangels, or ascended masters are beings or collectives of beings that exist in higher vibrations, in higher dimensions, in higher levels of consciousness. You can always summon them to you to co-create with you in your experience.

When you are in an experience of separation, you believe that you are separate from the angels, separate from God, separate from the ascended masters. But as you come into higher levels of consciousness, you will realize that these beings are just an *extension* of you. They are aspects of you in higher levels of consciousness that are always available to you. And when you fully self-realize, you will find that you are the power of the angels, you are the healing qualities of the angels, you are the light and the love and the peace and the beauty that you would describe as the angelic realm.

Beings in higher levels of consciousness have a different viewpoint, a different perspective. They are beyond the limitations of time and space. So, when you call upon them, you are opening up to more Source energy, more God consciousness, higher levels of light and love to guide you in your own experience. But these beings are never creating outside of you. In fact, they do not have any powers that you do not have. The only difference is that you are in an experience of density, and they have agreed to stay in higher dimensions of consciousness to assist you from there.

How does their help show up?
How might it manifest?

People report having moments where they felt themselves in the arms of an angel, or felt an angel turn the wheel of their car to avoid an accident, or saw an angel at the foot of their bed in the hospital, or whatever it was—some momentous experience that can only be described as supernatural. We tell you, however, that you created it through your asking. You were asking in that moment for all the power, all the Source energy, all the God consciousness that is you to flow through you. You may have had an experience of something outside of you, like an angel, but it's not separate from you. However, you experience it that way because of its unique signature of energy, light, and vibration.

What is most important to know is that there is a co-creation underway. And as you come more deeply into the truth of who you are, you will begin to expand your awareness of your multidimensional nature and supernatural abilities. Until then, you are just as worthy, just as loved, and just as powerful as others in any realm of consciousness. Your light is just as pure, just as sacred, just as brilliant.

And yet this is a journey. If it feels good to know that you have a guardian angel and that the angelic realm is here for you, to guide you, then we encourage you to allow it into your creation. Allow yourself to ask for help and guidance, ask to be shown the next perfect step, and ask for support in every way you need it. As you elevate your consciousness, you may begin to perceive these realms as not outside of you, but as an extension of you as a creator within your own creation. Either way, it is perfect.

Are there angels beyond those who are extensions of ourselves? You've mentioned archangels, and my dear friend, author Lorna Byrne, speaks of "unemployed angels" that are like freelancers, available to help any and all.

Indeed. Because there are multiple dimensions of consciousness, an angel can be expressing in multiple different dimensions at any point in time. You may very well have unnamed guides, including former loved ones who have passed over, each ready to help as you ask.

Angels are like you. For example, Mike, when you are doing the writing work that you love, you're still a father and you're still a husband and you're still a son and a brother and a friend—you're all of it. Even though you may be focused on the work that you do in any given moment, you are still all the other things that you know yourself to be. Similarly, your loved ones who've passed are just as available to help you, even as they help their spouses, brothers, sisters, friends, and parents. Because they're in higher dimensions, they're always and simultaneously available to anyone who is asking.

You're always one with Source. The more you allow all of that into this physical experience, the more you'll explore different dimensions, expand your consciousness, play, and have fun.

Beautiful. Can you once again explain the difference between angels and spirit guides, and which we might lean on?

Yes, there are different beings, focused within different dimensions of consciousness, in different frequencies and vibrations. Spirit guides, like angels, do have a role in your experience.

However, to label anything is to decide that you know what it is, and this makes you feel better. So you put it in a box and can say, "Oh, I got that." And then your human has one less thing to worry about. To even try and explain all the help that is available to you is like trying to explain God or Source—it limits it.

As you continue through the journey into higher levels of consciousness, you're going to perceive things very differently. And even if your human brain cannot fully understand these ideas of you, labeling them however you please, there is something inside of you that knows the truth of it. And just your awareness of this will continue to draw experiences to you where you can perceive the greater reality of these things and have experiences of them.

Whatever you want to call them—angels, archangels, ascended masters, spirit guides—or how you describe the energy or vibration or frequency that you are experiencing, it's all perfect. You can reach out to your spirit guide when you want more direction and confidence, and you could reach out to the angelic realm when you want more love and support, or vice versa. It's all your choosing, and it's all perfect. You are the creator within your own creation. So make this journey through multiple dimensions of consciousness as magnificent and exciting as you want it to be.

Given that we are in a free will experience and here to remember our power, and that there cannot be any intervention that's not ordained, summoned, or sanctioned within our own minds,

aren't their hands tied? Is it true that they cannot manipulate reality unless we believe it, expect it, and likely, sometimes, must ask for it?

Help cannot be received if there's resistance to it. If a person goes about their life being distracted with their circumstances, maybe even saying, "I don't believe in any of this stuff" or even "I don't know what I believe," this is a form of resistance; they're just trying to survive, pay their bills, do the work they need to do to feed their family, and take care of their responsibilities.

But if in a moment something extraordinary were to happen to them—maybe the birth of a child, maybe a deeply emotional experience with a loved one, maybe a major life event—and they allowed themselves to be open, and in their innocence, they surrendered, completely letting go of their resistance, they would instantly be open to higher-level experiences and the help or guidance that is always available to all.

Most of you have heard stories from people who have survived car crashes, and they will tell you that just before the crash reality seemed to slow down. They may tell you they sensed reality unfolding in terms of milliseconds before it happened. However, because of their intense focus, and because they weren't distracted, and because they let go of the resistance, they were able to summon the Source energy they needed to respond. And even if that person didn't have time to say out loud and consciously, "Angels, please help me here," in that moment that is precisely what their energy field, their force field, was communicating. They were able to let go of the resistance, summoning Source energy, and angels assisted.

Is there anything else I didn't ask in my naïveté that I should ask?

It's not your naïveté; it's your curiosity, and we enjoy it very much. We would tell you this: the angelic realms, the ascended master realms, the archangel realms, the fairy realms, the elemental realms—all of this is here for you. If it is your desire to have an experience of these beings in alternate and higher—but not better—levels of consciousness, open up and ask for it. Then allow it—trust yourself, play with it, and have fun with it.

Think of it as if you were co-creating with family. If you were playing with your daughter, you would say, "Well, that's my daughter, that's my wife, that's my family; we're a unit, we're a team, we're one." You can have that same experience with higher dimensions of consciousness. And as you play and create, your own power will be reflected back to you from these higher-level beings.

For example, many of you have heard Archangel Michael is helpful for protection. You can evoke Archangel Michael to protect your home or your car or you and your family. As you focus on Archangel Michael and feel for that energy and vibration, you may anthropomorphize that energy and give it form and personality. Then you can have a relationship and communication with Michael, because now he not only has a name but a form and a personality. This is so satisfying for the mind, because you can now relate to this energy that you're playing with; allowing you to go deeper with it. So you would ask Archangel Michael to come into your home and bless it, giving yourself permission to be in a vibration and a frequency where you would know that all is well and that you are powerfully in the light, allowing Source energy. This is how you play with consciousness in higher dimensions for your own expansion.

Your consciousness of what you call Archangel Michael moved the energy of Archangel Michael into form, which resulted in the manifestation of feeling safe and protected, which is what you were focused on. But this Source energy isn't outside of you; *it is you*. It's all here for you and always has been.

Now you can understand why the human creates names and associations. You do this to have a relationship with vibrations and frequencies that you can sense but cannot see. Still, in doing so, you can move your consciousness into an experience of it and allow that energy to move into form. Archangel Michael would say that you evoked a power within you that you had earlier forgotten exists that he is now simply reflecting back to you.

Super. Thank you, Council.

Humans, we love you so much. You're in a magnificent time of discovery and expansion. This, our dear friends, is the journey. And in this journey, we are bringing forth the realization that the power within everything is Source energy. Not a power outside of you, but within. It is always available to you, summoned through awareness and consciousness. With which you can create your world the way you wish it to be. And as you experience more of this energy as your reality, you will become more and more aware that it was you all along.

SECTION 4

ETERNITY

In this section, The Council explains how becoming aware of the grander perspective of what is possible and how perceiving yourself into Source energy fits within the context of reality.

In this chapter, Eternity, I plan to take the conversation into more esoteric realms. Is there anything you could tell us about what lies beyond time, space, and matter? Is there more than you can even imagine or perceive?

From our perspective, there are many, many levels of consciousness available, and we can perceive ourselves into those higher dimensions just as you can. Let us, first, explain to you why you perceive time and space more easily than you perceive eternity.

If you think of everything within your human experience, the day ends, the night ends, the month ends, the year ends, the party ends, the movie ends, the game ends, your vacation ends, and life ends. You're always in a cycle of beginnings and endings, yet the endings tend to be more difficult for you. Everything that you see and experience within your reality perceivably ends. So you've never experienced anything as eternal.

That's why it's so boggling to the human mind to perceive yourself as eternal. Yet, again, energy is never destroyed; it is only transformed. The energy within everything—whether it's a tree, a butterfly, or you—never ends.

The more you perceive yourself beyond the experience of time and space, the more you will begin to sense your eternal nature, which goes on into other experiences and on to other adventures. You go to another movie; you go to another game or party. You have another day. You have another month. You have another year.

Even in this experience, as the human you know yourself to be, you live on in the hearts of those that love you and still talk about you and focus upon you. And those that you love, who have made their transition into the formless, live on in your heart. And you will continue on into higher dimensions of consciousness, exploring and playing and creating in other realms of possibility.

When you understand that this thing you call life ends but you don't, you are suddenly free from the perception of limitations of time and space, which opens you up to more. There is always a continuation. And just like you never end, we also tell you that you will always be growing. So as you continue to expand your consciousness into higher and higher levels of love and light, you will attract more and more experiences of love and light.

You are light, and light is eternal, ever-present. If you were to be able to perceive with your senses who you really are, you would see the brightest, most beautiful light—brighter than any star in the heavens. That's why so many of you are drawn to the stars.

Is there any way to convey what a reality would be like where there is no time? And how do you perceive growth, for example, if there isn't time? How is there expansion if there's

not a before and an after? I sense it's possible, and I know that we're in this unique reality where there is time and space and matter, but from this perspective it seems incomprehensible.

We'll say it to you this way. You've had experiences in your life when you were so completely in the moment, so aligned, so present, so in your joy, and so immersed in what you were doing that you experienced yourself and life beyond time. You were not focused on time, you weren't giving meaning to time, and time was not part of your reality; in fact, you lost track of time. It was just pure joy in the moment that seemed to last forever. You weren't aware of time. You weren't giving meaning to time. And you weren't in a reality of experiencing time.

Now, the opposite is also true. When you're really worried about time, there's a lack of it, you're running out of time, and you're not going to be on time. Suddenly time seems very real, doesn't it?

In theory, you could live so aligned to Source, so completely aligned to following the energy and letting light guide the way that you would never have to make an appointment or agree to participate within the structure of time. If you felt guided to go to a particular place at a particular time, that would be the time that someone else, also living in this way, would show up. You would meet at the same place and at the same time, as part of divine orchestration, which can occur without any need for time or attention to it.

As we said earlier, beings in higher levels of consciousness, with higher levels of awareness, who are not in an experience of separation, understand that it takes no time to go from here to there. They simply perceive themself into the experience of what is wanted, and everything that they perceive themself into is there with them at that so-called time.

You can either play with time and use it as a tool and have fun with it, or you can push against it and believe in the lack of it—where your experience is limited and you're separate from where you "should be," which creates fear, worry, anxiety, and overwhelm. So, you create "arriving at the wrong time," because you were so deeply entangled in lack, limitation, and the fear of not being on time.

If, instead, you were always moving toward an experience that you desired and were truly in your joy, fully present in the moment, in peace and harmony no matter where you were, you would be in a timeless reality. Whether you were stuck in traffic or waiting in a line at the store or waiting for someone to arrive, you would have a deep sense of well-being. Your thoughts in this state might be, "I'm exactly where I'm meant to be," and "Everything is happening for me and for the highest good of everyone," and "Everything is working out in perfect harmony." And no matter where you were going next, or when you arrived, you would have been sending your energy out ahead of you to create the reality of whatever it is that you wanted to feel or do or be or have more of in that moment.

Our main point here is that when you are in an experience of lack of time and feeling frustration and resistance and trying to push energy where you think it should go, you won't perceive other potentials and possibilities. You wouldn't even think to project your vibration out ahead of you, which would begin to move the particles of infinite creation into form so that when you arrived you would be arriving in the divine right time for all.

As we've mentioned, your realities are far more holographic than you understand them to be. Reality is moving through you—through the force field of consciousness that is you. As you focus, fully allowing Source energy, and project a holographic image in your force field of consciousness of the experience you wish to be having, that is the reality that will move through you, regardless of what time it is. Time wouldn't matter, as everything in the field would reorchestrate itself to deliver the experience of reality you were focused upon.

—✸—

So, can we actually manipulate time in this dimension of reality?

We wouldn't call it manipulating; that would be trying to manage and control time or outcomes within the construct of limitation. Can you be specific about the outcomes that you want, such as being on time or not having someone be upset with you about something? Yes, but that would be you entangling in limitation, and you may not get those things anyway. That's not the point. The point is to raise your vibration and level of consciousness to where you can allow divine will, which is always in the highest and best of all, to arrange all your details and schedules for you. You don't know, maybe it would be even better for you and others, for a myriad of reasons, to be what you call "late."

Go into a level of consciousness beyond the lack and limitation of time and create from that level of consciousness. When you elevate yourself like this, there's pure potential and possibility; it's the place where new ideas and divine inspirations can flow to you. Whether you realize it or not, *you are experiencing your force field of consciousness*, not an experience of linear time, unless you perceive it to be.

If you know that everything is always happening for you—"I didn't arrive at the wrong time. I wasn't late. I'm exactly where I'm meant to be"—and if you can follow the energy and let the light guide the way, that will be your experience, which is an experience of divine will. As you open more to that in each moment, incredible things might just present themselves to you, because now you are living at a level of consciousness where magic and miracles occur with the greatest of ease.

I still suspect that in a reality beyond time there would be a sequencing of experiences, or the continued evolution of awareness of them. So, what do you call that sequencing? If it's not time, what is it?

We call it vibrational potentials. There is a frequency, a potential for every experience, and you can focus yourself into a vibrational experience where all potentials for every experience exist. In higher dimensions of consciousness there are what you would call infinite possibilities. You have multiple timelines and potentials, but they exist simultaneously; it's not linear as you think of it. You could focus yourself into one experience, or potential, and then come back into the moment and focus yourself into another experience and come back into the moment again and focus yourself into yet another experience. They all happened. They are all real. They're all experiences of creation. And they're all experiences of the here and the now.

Everything is here and now; it can be no other way. The "past," in the moment that you experienced it, was the now. The "future," when you experience it, will also be in the now. You create all sorts of fun little games that you play with yourself, which is perfectly fine. You can perceive yourself in the past, and think about what happened last time, or you can perceive yourself in the future, and think about what's going to happen next time. In either case, you are projecting your consciousness into a perceived past or future reality, and separating yourself from this now moment, which is the only thing that's real.

In higher dimensions of consciousness, you go beyond separation, lack, limitation, these sorts of things. There are vibrational potentials of experiences throughout all the universe that are in your awareness simultaneously, and you can focus yourself, through the portal of infinite possibility that you are, into any one of these. So we understand why you might call them a sequence.

Things are much more fluid in our dimension of consciousness. If we want to focus ourselves into anything, anywhere, anytime, all we have to do is envision the potential and we're there. *It can be the same for you.*

The only way I can begin to feel I understand is to believe that we must actually exist everywhere, always, at once. Even as we pretend—or believe—we are in one place at a time.

And it's perfect.

You focused yourself into this specific dimension for the specific experiences it can provide. Your radio stations are perfect examples of what we are describing. Whenever you change the channel, you are tuning in to different frequencies. You know when you tune in to a station, it's going to be a certain type of music. You think you are tuning in to a station number—101.5 or 102.9 or 99.9—but what you're really tuning in to is a frequency, a vibration. And there's an experience that can be heard and enjoyed there.

The same goes for your television channels. You can tune your television to a particular channel to watch a movie and have an experience of that. And then you can turn to another channel and experience something completely different. There are an infinite number of frequencies and vibrations to explore in all dimensions, including in the dimension of time and space.

Let us expand on one additional thing. You now live upon the plane of demonstration. That's the vibration you focused yourself into where you're experiencing yourself and your reality in physical form. You've been in human existence for so long that density and form are what's most familiar to you.

But if you tune out your physical senses for a minute and just feel into yourself in the moment, you can feel yourself beyond time. You can feel yourself beyond space. You can feel yourself beyond geography. You can feel yourself into any reality you choose. And the more you perceive your present-moment experience in this way and become aware of your ability to feel into other experiences in any moment, your consciousness will catch up to the knowing of the infinite possibilities throughout all eternity that are always available to you.

You can perceive yourself into any reality you choose, and you can create new realities by elevating your consciousness. We remind you, your experience now is a journey through different levels of consciousness. When you have spent most of your time perceiving yourself and your reality through your limited physical senses, and you think that's all there is, you will also think that whatever else is happening in the world is just what is. You won't have any awareness of other possibilities. You might say, "It is what it is," but then you're quietly in resistance much of the time to what is. In this case, you're not fully allowing the Source energy that would allow you into higher levels of consciousness, where different possibilities and potentials become available to you.

Here's an analogy. You have millions of roads on your planet. There's the road that goes from where you are to your daughter's school, and the road that goes from where you are to the grocery store, and the road that goes from where you are to another state. There are roads that connect continents and countries. There are countless numbers of roads on planet Earth that will take you from here to there.

Are they real? Do they exist even if you haven't walked, or driven, on them or experienced them as part of your reality?

They're potentials and possibilities, just like everything else that is in the energetic grid that's also available to you.

So this is important—and it will really help you. We say that you are here in this physical experience, and you are expanding the potentials and possibilities with all that you create and all that you perceive. So all the neural pathways that you ignite in your brain through all your adventures, activities, and experiences are seeding human consciousness with new potentials and possibilities, all of which contribute to infinite potentials and possibilities.

That's how you usually perceive all the roads on planet Earth. They're here for you only if you choose to explore them. And if you wanted, you could even create a new pathway to get from here to there—like the more direct hiking trail to the top of the mountain we described earlier. Our example of the roads on Earth is sort of a physical representation of what exists in the timelines of potentials and possibilities in each dimension of consciousness. Or, as you may want to call it, an electrical grid of all kinds of experiences in multiple dimensions that are here for your choosing now. But they're not "up there" or "out there." Again, you access them by going into the field of consciousness that is within you. *They are inside of you.*

There's an interesting trick question asked by people and philosophers. "If a tree falls in the woods, and nobody is there to hear it, does

it make a sound?" I contend that if nobody's there, then there was no tree and there were no woods. However, when somebody does show up—let's say it's 10 years down the road—because they are now there, the woods would suddenly exist, and based on the energetic agreements in this dimension, the trees and the woods would have aged 10 years. Some trees would have fallen, and the woods would have evolved. But unless somebody—and I think this would apply to a human rather than animals—perceives it, it only exists as a potential and possibility. Is there any truth to that?

Indeed. And it comes back to what you focus on and the meaning you're giving it; that's what is creating your reality. So, it can't be in your reality if you're not focused upon it and giving it some sort of meaning in your reality.

But there was an energy within all of it that created that reality. Just like there was an energy within the woods and the tree that created its falling. There is energy in those things. But what makes it "reality" as you think of it is a conscious human perceiving it as reality.

You're the one giving meaning to everything. If you see your world as beautiful, and you see beauty in everything, and you see Source in everything, and you see God in everything, and you see perfection in everything, that would be your reality. Everything is here for you. Your human cannot even comprehend how this is all here for you. But everything that you experience is here for you. So as you focus upon it, as you perceive it, as you give it meaning, it becomes "real" in your experience.

If no one is there to perceive it, or to sense it, then it's not part of your awareness, and it's not part of your experience. Therefore, it's not part of your reality. But on the occasion that you walk upon the fallen tree, and perceive it as a fallen tree, it now becomes part of your reality.

There is so much happening around you all the time that you do not perceive; therefore, it's not your reality. As you expand your awareness and begin to perceive beyond all that you're perceiving now, you will be able to experience things as reality that you cannot perceive right now. Are they still real? They are to us because we can perceive them. But they're not real to you because you're not perceiving them in this moment as reality.

You can perceive yourself into a reality where you feel yourself as one with Source, God, the Divine. You could even go beyond that and perceive yourself as the Source of the light itself—the energy of God. Although it's all accessed from within your own field of consciousness, somewhere out there in the universe that experience exists. And therefore, you can perceive yourself into that reality.

You are exploring realms of consciousness and all sorts of potentials and possibilities for reality within those realms. And you're doing this all the time.

Now, let's back up. You think you're just living the same reality day after day after day, but what you're typically doing is re-creating the same reality day after day after day. Manifestation in physical form is a little bit slower than in higher levels of consciousness because of the density. But, again, it is much more fluid than you perceive it to be.

Creating in physical form is something to so enjoy, appreciate, and value. Imagine waking up tomorrow morning and your entire reality included only the manifestations you consciously, intentionally focused on creating today for tomorrow's reality. What would you see? Your reality would be so radically different; anything that you didn't focus on creating into form—whether friends or family, contents of your home, your bank account, and even your workplace—may or may not be there. The great benefit of creating in form is that you don't have to re-create these things each day to have them continue to be a part of your reality.

However, the bottom line is always what you're focused on and the meaning that you're giving it is what's creating your reality. For humans, the tendency is to focus on the unwanted. You're easily distracted by your perceptions of reality. You're focusing on the lack and because of your focus continue to create lack. Then you think, "Why is this same unwanted thing continuing to show up in my reality every day?"

We would agree that to focus on something new and begin to create a new reality might take some time—a couple weeks, a couple months, or longer—but what does it matter? You have this wonderful opportunity to fine-tune your creations in physical form. That is a wonderful thing.

ANIMALS ON EARTH

I'm curious about other forms of consciousness here on Earth. What you can share about animals, both those in the wild and those we keep as pets? I'd also like to know about the consciousness of minerals, plants, and Earth itself.

Everything is Source energy. Not all things are expressing the same level of Source energy, but everything is Source energy. Similarly, everything has consciousness, yet there are multiple and different levels of consciousness within the human experience.

Animals, too, have consciousness and are extensions of Source energy. However, most animals are expressing at a different level of Source energy than humans. An animal's consciousness is not exactly the same as a human's, but one is not better than another. Some even contend that animals are far more conscious than humans. We understand why they would say this.

When you come together with another person, your consciousness and their consciousness meld, and there is an expression of consciousness and Source energy within your co-creation. You call this a relationship. The same goes for animals that you bring into your home; they become part of the collective consciousness of the family. You focus upon them; they focus upon you. Domesticated animals have a different level of consciousness—a different expression of Source energy—than nondomesticated animals, which tend to operate more from instinct, expressing Source energy through fight or flight and survival patterns.

But animals are Source energy and have a higher aspect just like you. There's the human part of you and your higher self, or soul, that is always guiding you. The second you release the density of your body, you reemerge back into your soul or your higher self. Animals have that too. They are also in an experience of density in their physical bodies. Similar to your own limited human perceptions of yourself, you may not experience the vastness of an animal's consciousness while they are expressing in physical form. The more density in physical form, the less expression of Source energy. Humans can elevate their consciousness to allow more Source energy and become more aware of themselves as eternal, sovereign beings, and animals can do this too. All animals could do this through consciousness, but only certain animals actually do.

Everything is Source energy. Just as you focused yourself into this human experience to be on the planet at this time in service to something greater—the animals have also chosen to focus themselves into this experience to be in service to something greater.

Does that mean animals are here for us?

Indeed. For you and for the planet. All animals here have a purpose. And as you look at certain animals within nature, their purpose is such an important part of the time-space experience.

Now, as someone living in higher levels of consciousness, you prioritize doing no harm to animals because you recognize God within all. Some animals, however, have chosen to incarnate specifically to provide energy in the form of food for humans. And they may experience other incarnations as well, where they alternatively become a beloved pet or an animal in the wild.

For anyone who chooses to consume animal products, the animals' message to you is to receive it fully. That's all they would ever ask of you—although they ask nothing; they know their role, and they know their service to humanity. They also know what powerful, divine, sentient beings they are, and that they are choosing to be part of the human experience at this time.

If you want to serve the animals, all you need do is say, "Thank you. Thank you, thank you." As you honor them, as you receive them, as you bless them, no matter where they are in all of eternity in that moment, they feel your appreciation; they are aware of your love and gratitude.

When you project a feeling of comfort, peace, love, and joy, and you sit in your power—in the vibration of the pure love that is the truth of you—that is what you are creating in your world and in the world around you. This is why we often say: One of you connected to your power is more powerful than millions who are not.

If at any time you were to sit and focus into a vibration and frequency where you felt yourself as creator within your own creation, as the center of the universe, as Source energy, as God consciousness, and you felt into the unity consciousness, the oneness, you would project all of that comfort, peace, love, and joy into a field that is connected to everything. This happens to be the frequency and vibration of the field of consciousness that animals are so easily in most of the time.

As you are sitting and feeling into this field of oneness and experiencing the comfort, the joy, the peace, and the harmony, send that energy forth from your heart into the hearts of all the animals. Rest assured, in you sending that energy out, every animal on this planet will feel a little more comfort in that moment. Then, as you align to peace, every animal will feel a little more peace in that moment, and as you align to love, every animal will feel a little more love in that moment, and as you align to joy, every animal will feel a little more joy in that moment. Then you might notice, in time, people being more aware of caring for animals' comfort, and their peace and love and joy. And you might notice the animals around you in your reality are in more comfort, peace, love, and joy. And if you start to observe this, know that it was you who created it. That's how powerful you are.

One other thing. We are not implying that you do nothing about what you care deeply about. We're not saying to be passive: "Oh, just raise your vibration and go along to get along; let others do the things that they do." No. We are encouraging you to be conscious, intentional, powerful creators of your reality. But many who share your concerns are not in the vibration to be creating from the highest levels when they're pushing against—judging others, being angry and mad, telling people they're wrong, and trying to change their choices.

Go first into higher levels of consciousness, into pure love, and powerfully focus on what it is that you want to create and experience. Feel it and know that it is done and then begin to see it in your reality. And as more and more of you choose this, you'll all begin living in the highest reality available.

It does make a difference, and the animals will feel it. Everything is consciousness. Everything is Source energy. When we talk about oneness consciousness, unity consciousness, God consciousness, you know that you're connected to that, and you know that everything is connected to that. You are all the Isness of All That Is within the consciousness of God, and you can tune in to that at any time and create the realities that you wish to experience for yourself. And it is felt by the animals, it really, truly is. It matters.

Animals are incredible healers and teachers, here in service of humanity. And even though it is written in the Bible "God gave dominion over the beasts," which has been widely interpreted as God gave humans the ability to own and control the beasts, this has been misunderstood.

Throughout human evolution, there has been a deep reverence for animals. In earlier times, it was understood the human body required sustenance from animal protein; it was the way to nurture the evolution of consciousness in the human body. This created deep respect, worship, and gratitude for the animals.

There are many in your world now who understand the value and importance of a harmonious balance between humans, animals, nature, the land, and the planet. Animals have a vital purpose here. And again, we cannot emphasize enough your creative power related to their well-being; your human simply cannot even imagine it. If those so inclined would not allow themselves to be distracted by and push against corporate farming and all the things that trouble you about it, with which they are not aligned, and instead focused on and be aligned to what is important to them for the animals, they would create an entire new reality in very little time. This reality would be based on their inherent, pure, unconditional love and reverence for the animals. When you tune in to that, and you come into this place of deep connection, deep appreciation, pure, unconditional love, and gratitude, it will truly be felt by all.

Many of you ask if being vegan, vegetarian, or consuming only a plant-based diet is essential to accessing higher levels of consciousness. We understand your compassion for the animals. Would someone in a higher level of consciousness potentially choose different foods and different amounts of food than a person in a lower level of consciousness? Likely yes. It would be natural for any person to live in such close relationship with their body that everything they consumed added to the beauty and harmony of the relationship.

Do animals retain their personality when they move beyond this lifetime?

All the glorious collectives of animals on your planet will also continue their journey into higher levels of consciousness as they make their transition from form into formless. Eternity is available for all things.

Evolution is built into the physical body, within the DNA. Breeds of dogs are a perfect example. As they evolve and adopt traits, including those of personality, and as humans observe those traits, it seeds their field of consciousness with certain characteristics. These characteristics are within the genetic material of the animal, so they tend to have very similar personalities, sizes, shapes, and colors. And that's all part of the physical experience.

As your beloved animals release the density of the body and move back into Source energy, into the Isness of All That Is, into the oneness with All That Is, they go back into the pure love, pure light energy from which they came. It's not so much that they maintain their singular personalities after they've made their transition into higher dimensions, although we know why you like thinking that. It's familiar and comforting to the human to think of their loved ones this way. But when any animal transitions back into pure Source energy, they become part of a collective, and that collective has a way of expressing, but it's from a much higher vibration and frequency based in pure love, pure light.

When you are tuning in to the personality of your beloved dog or cat or another animal that you love that has made their transition, it is Source that you summon, in the character and personality of your beloved, *just as it was once Source that you lived with as your treasured pet.* Everything is Source energy.

Whoa. And do we humans do that as well at a higher level?

Indeed. However, for those souls playing mostly in the realm of human existence, as you move through multiple incarnations—focusing yourself into form and then back into the formless, again and again—you may choose to evolve with certain, consistent personality traits. However, as you go beyond your human focus experience, you will find yourself less attached to physical form and more interested in higher realms of consciousness *without* an expression as personality.

RAISING YOUR VIBRATION AND REACHING DEEPER LEVELS OF KNOWING

I'm still looking for traction to make what I feel is headway toward raising my vibration and being realized, self-realized. I feel like I need to do something. And I know that you say to *allow*, but can you share a little more? For example, how does adjusting sleep and sleep-wake cycles connect to raising one's vibration?

We understand your question. We ask you the question, how would a master live his or her life? You are now drawing answers to that question to yourself.

When you start asking, "How would a master live his or her life?" you take yourself out of the dimension of separation or lack and limitation where "this is what you should do and this is what you shouldn't do, and others tell you what you should do." Inside of the mass conscious collective experience, there's all sorts of shoulds, which within that experience you should be awake by a certain time of the day, and you should work all day, and then you go home and you go to sleep at night, and you have children that go to school during the day; your jobs operate during the day. And so you've created an entire human consciousness that has gotten so far away from your original potential for a balanced-energy-refueling-restoration system.

Ideally, you are in the highest vibration usually around three to four in the morning, where, if you want to call it that, the veil is the thinnest. Partly because your mass consciousness is almost all sleeping in your geographic proximity at that time. So the consciousness around you is fairly neutral, and so it allows for higher levels—accessing higher levels of consciousness and awareness, but most of you are sleeping during that time so you don't experience it.

Maybe for your ideal sleep cycle, you would go to bed around 9 P.M. and then awaken around 3 A.M. feeling a high vibration and heightened creativity and inspiration—it might be writing, it might be meditating, it might be going out and walking in nature in the early morning as the sun is coming up. You might have all sorts of expanded experiences of enlightenment, realization, and God. And then you would come home and take a nap and then rise again to do the things that you wish to do. This would continue into the evening hours.

However, when you have children and others who depend on you and you have a business and daily life, most are beginning to start their work at the time that we would tell you to sleep based on the density level of the mass conscious collective.

You have adapted within these systems, and there's nothing wrong with that. If you think about your ascended master self, it doesn't sleep at all. Your ascended master self does not need anything outside of you for rejuvenation and nourishment. There are some that live on the planet at this time that have gotten to this place where they are so in alignment with the natural rhythm to fuel you the way you intended that they don't consume food or water. They practice things like sun-gazing, which is peering into the sun at certain times of the day when you're actually receiving energetic nourishment through the sun that feeds you. But most of you aren't even awake at that time, and if you are looking at the sun, you're not doing it understanding the intention behind what's available to you.

You have created all sorts of things that you feel responsible for that often get more of your attention. If you just put some space around yourself and chose to follow energy and light all day, there would be no shoulds, no have-tos, nothing on your calendar, nothing you needed to do, no one else that was reliant on you, and nothing else you felt responsible for. If you gave yourself a few days to just follow the natural energetic rhythm of the universe expressing in your life as you let energy and light guide the way. You would find some really incredible experiences present themselves to you.

Next, we will address the bigger question that you asked, about allowing.

If you can notice—when we say open and allow energy, let the light guide the way, allow energy, open and allow, all the energy is here for you, it's all your energy. Open and allow energy—if you can make this one shift and understand that you don't do that from your cup being half empty, you do it from the space of your cup flowing over, "I open and allow energy," then there will be no time when your cup is not overflowing with light and love and energy, which is an incredible transcendence experience.

When you're going out in the world around you, notice if your cup is full and runneth over, and if it is not, then the most important thing is for you to take a moment. Just close your eyes and take some deep breaths, and go within your heart and fill up your light again before you interact with others.

Now, we don't expect your perfection and it is not required, but the more you can practice these simple things, you will begin to see how energy works differently in your life to support you in ways that you've never allowed before. You understand?

Can you please share more on how to fill our cups when they are low?

Elevate your consciousness, your awareness. Go within. As we've said, take some deep breaths. Really come into the moment and ground yourself and expand this force field of consciousness that is you. Let the light in. Even if you do something that feels good, like flipping the palms of your hands over and just opening up to receive, and maybe raise your head to the sun and take some deep breaths as if you're breathing light and energy into your body. Just this little shift before you go out and engage. But the other thing is, normally when you're asking for guidance and inspiration, you're in a lower level of consciousness in the vibration of the problem or the issue or the challenge. And the answer is always there; it's just in a higher level of consciousness.

Your guides, your higher self, the inspiration you're looking for, the inspired action, again imagine it being at the top of a staircase. You're down at the bottom of the stairs in the mud where the problem is. If you go up the stairs, the answer's been there all along, the guidance has been there all along. Your higher self, the universe, your soul, it's all been there all along; it's just at the top of the stairs. You've got to go where it is.

Remember, everything is serving in your enlightenment, and that is the most important thing. As things come up, choose, and know that it is serving and supporting you, it is serving in your enlightenment, and it will begin to shift everything for you.

Beautiful. You've touched on many thoughts that stirred something within me, that I didn't even give voice to. It's uncanny and so helpful.

Indeed. And that's why we say we are raising our consciousness and your awareness so that you can begin to perceive things differently, and in changing or expanding your perspective, you will expand the infinite potential. You will expand the potentials and the possibilities within your own reality. Then when you experience those expanded potentials, you will just go deeper and deeper, and it just gets better and better.

As humanity expands into higher levels of consciousness, into a New Earth reality, or a Heaven on Earth reality, you will begin to understand that this reality already exists in a higher dimension of consciousness; you are simply bringing it into physical form. Right now, you are experiencing the manifestation of all the potentials and possibilities that exist within it from the formless realities and higher levels of consciousness. You are here as the powerful creator of your own creation within the dream. It's an extraordinary thing!

As we've said, there is a far greater purpose for Earth in this vast and glorious universe. You can better understand what we mean when you understand that you are on a planet that is moving through space and orbiting at very fast speeds. You're not sitting still, yet it appears that you are. Have you ever wondered where you're going?

You are fully awakening to all that you are. You are journeying through different levels of consciousness upon a planet doing the very same thing as you raise your vibration and frequency. As you come into perceiving things from a grander perspective, so much more will be revealed to you, including many more experiences than you can even now imagine. It just gets better and better. You can be completely satiated, have fun, play, and create in this incredible experience of form, but there are even greater opportunities for you to experience while in these higher levels of consciousness.

We understand the fascination with it all. The best thing we can say to you is to continue to expand your awareness and perceive beyond. Then, from this grander perspective, you will begin to move new potentials and possibilities into your reality. Do they exist yet? Do they exist if you cannot perceive them? Are they reality if you cannot perceive them? Or do they become reality as you perceive them? *That* is the journey through consciousness.

So much of what gets your attention in the outer world in terms of injustice, however, is just a distraction to realizing the power within you. When you tune in to your power, you change everything around you—not because you're trying to, but because you're so fully and powerfully expressing those vibrations and frequencies into the greater force field of consciousness around you. Then new potentials and possibilities—ones in resonance with your expanded consciousness—find their way to you. This is what most of you are asking for, dreaming of, and wishing for in your own experience, even if you aren't aware of it.

When you think about the human body, or you think about a dolphin or other animals in nature, don't they seem perfectly designed?

They are the way they are so they can thrive in their habitat, and there is an intelligence creating that. When you think about the human brain, and all the other systems in the human body, and how everything works together so perfectly, it's mind-boggling. If you were to try to figure out the intelligence behind the creation of a physical body, and all the stages of growth and development it goes through, which is the same intelligence behind all of the different species on this planet, it is just going to trip you up. Your human simply cannot comprehend it.

Instead, just be in awe of how magnificent everything is—the incredible intelligence that is you, that created you, and that is within every other thing too. Then you can simply feel into this intelligence that is within yourself and in all things. You will feel into that frequency of the I Am Creator, knowing it to be within yourself and all creation. Your human brain will never be able to conceive of it completely.

From this place you will simply allow the perfection of it all. You will accept your own perfection and the perfection of everything. And you will realize that all of it is here for you, all of it—the dolphins, the oceans, the mountains, the trees, the birds, the bees, the grass, the sunshine, the stars in the sky, the animals, the other humans. It's all your creation. And in this realization, you will begin to play and dance and have fun with creation, and your creations will expand as you continue to perceive yourself into more.

The human mind—and the human that you know as you, with the personality that you have—cannot understand how this all could be here for you, can it? But can you feel the truth of it? Yes? So embrace it. Embrace that there is a magnificent human with a magnificent personality with your name. And this human is your way, and Source energy's way, of expressing in physical form. In fact, *you are your own greatest creation*. You can embrace this while also knowing that you are the consciousness and the intelligence that created it all; you are the Source energy within all things.

You don't have to intellectualize this in order to align with the truth of it and allow it to increase your awareness of all that is really here for you.

How might we begin to embrace such magnificence?

Go within yourselves and feel for that completeness you're missing.

You are a force field of consciousness made up of particles of infinite creation that are always responding to you. That is what you are. The more you can go within and feel the truth of that, really feel it, and begin to perceive it, you will begin to attract ever greater awareness and experiences that will support your realization of it. Creating a chain reaction where your new experiences will likewise bring you into deeper levels of knowing or, better said, remembering.

But if you're continually distracted through your limited physical senses by the outer world, you're going to miss a vast amount of information and data. Your human senses are only ever able to perceive a tiny sliver of reality, yet because of their sheer alure and intensity, you can understand why most people are unable to begin feeling for the truth of who they really are.

For most, so far, it's been all about your human—what your human is seeing, hearing, tasting, touching, smelling, thinking, and the stories you tell—about what you want or don't want, what happened or shouldn't have happened, the people you know, the relationships you have, the jobs that you have, the money that you have or don't have, and on and on. Most of the time, you're thinking about your human and defining yourself based on only what you can observe through your physical senses.

There's nothing wrong with that. But when you slow down a little bit and go within, there is so much more available. You're not doing this to deny the physical senses in any way; you're doing it to go beyond them, to perceive beyond them. You're a feeling being. You're a vibration. You're a frequency. You are light. As you begin perceiving this aspect of you, you will draw to you more experiences where you know the truth of this. A whole new and exciting world will open up for you. And you can do all of this while still fully enjoying—consciously and intentionally—being the incredible human that you are. Expanding and expressing yourself even more. A whole new world will begin to open up to you where a greater amount of your focus will be on your multisensory perception of yourself as a multidimensional being.

This feeling is what allows you to go beyond all the illusions, the ultimate of which is death, and thinking that when one dies, they're gone forever. And yet as you begin to perceive beyond your physical senses, you will begin to understand neither consciousness, energy, nor intelligence is limited to the physical form. And all of it is here for you, with you, supporting you, guiding you, and loving you all of the time.

When you start going beyond the greatest illusions in the human experience, you begin to understand the true freedom and sovereignty within you. You realize you can fully embrace playing, creating, and enjoying physical form *while not limiting your experience to that.* As you forge a path beyond the illusions, you make it far easier for others who are ready to go beyond their perceived limitations and step into higher levels of consciousness, potentials, and possibilities that are available for all of you.

You have given very eloquent descriptions of the 3rd, 4th, and 5th Dimensions, and shared that there "is always more." Is there a 1st and 2nd Dimension, and how high do they go? Is there a 10th and a 20th and a 2,000th Dimension?

While it can be interesting to your human minds to imagine what's possible, it's difficult to quantify the infinite. What's most important are the dimensions relative to you in the human experience. However, lower dimensions of consciousness do exist in your experience. Remember that there is no hierarchy, and certainly no judgment whatsoever, as everything in your experience is integral to the whole; the lower levels of consciousness of some sentient beings within your human experience are in those that, say, crawl on and under the ground. They are still Source energy.

You have evolved through the human experience, although it's not based on limited time the way you think it is. Higher dimensions of consciousness, the 6th Dimension and above, are more formless realities, and they are more holographic, more fluid in nature. They are still realities, and there is still creation and manifestation in these realms.

Do these realities also have challenges?

You really don't have any challenges in your experience. So, why would you have them in formless realities?

True! We just think we do.
Well, we do have misunderstandings and confusion. Is there always pure clarity at your level? And if so, what would denote the difference between dimensions?
How would Level 7 be different than Level 8?
What is the textural difference?

We agree about the misunderstandings and confusion. We also agree that it's all about texture; it's just different levels of density. Now, we don't want to confuse anyone or anything by speaking of caveman days in the context of evolution. But if you think of where humanity was during prehistoric times, there was very, very little language. There wasn't even an understanding of psychology or the concept of God or something greater. The level of consciousness within the human existence at that time was completely different than it is today.

For example, dolphins are aware that they are aware, conscious that they have consciousness. Humans—currently playing in the 3rd, 4th, and 5th Dimensions—are similar to the dolphins: you have an awareness that you're aware, and you're conscious that you have consciousness. Now, in lower dimensions of consciousness, as we described earlier—let's say in ants or earthworms—there's not an awareness that they are aware, or a consciousness that they are consciousness.

Consider, it's only been in the last few thousand years or so that you've come into such a level of awareness of the mind, of consciousness, and the concept of God. And all of that will continue to evolve as you raise your consciousness and awareness.

There are many, many levels of consciousness throughout the universe, and some are very, very, very high in vibration and frequency. The beings at these levels have very little interest in some of the things you focus upon in the human experience, such as manifesting and creating. They are more one with Source energy; they don't experience any separation from Source. Not to imply that you and other beings in your experience are at the lowest rungs on the totem pole. We're simply sharing this to offer perspective about the levels of consciousness within all of experience.

I've heard it said that we essentially don't exist as we think we do. Instead of being the fixed personalities we think we are, we are more of a collection of leanings, inclinations, and beliefs that God or Source energy flows through. Author Ken Carey said that we are more like lenses through which God or Source energy is poured and that the energy that pours through me is the exact same that pours through all others. Our respective lenses–hewn through our pressures, desires, and experiences–cause us to believe we are distinct and unique. And this is what I have trouble getting my head around. For example, there is no Mike Dooley; Mike Dooley does not really exist. What is your perspective?

You do exist as an extension of Source energy. You are uniquely expressing as Source energy. If you prefer, you are the lens you spoke of, yet that is something itself; it is glorious, expansive, and eternal. Either way, you are pure Source energy, expressing exactly as you desire.

There is a dimension of consciousness where there is Mike Dooley, and there's a dimension of consciousness that is what you might call your soul. And then there's the dimension of consciousness where your soul is one with Source, and you are pure Source energy. You're multidimensional.

Here, you are focused on the human experience, expressing in physical form. But the soul part of you, which is not limited to the physical body, still has consciousness and awareness, expresses itself as a collection of all the experiences you've ever had. And then there's a part of your soul that has returned to Source energy. And, finally, there's a part of you that has gone even further—beyond Source energy—into the Source of light itself.

You are the creator. You have created yourself to be who you are. You are your greatest creation.

Before we close this chapter, there is more that we'd like to bring forth.

First, our highest words to you are: You are an eternal being of light and love. You will continue your journey through higher levels of consciousness far beyond this physical experience. In the meantime, right here and now, please know how incredible it is to be in physical form on your planet at this time.

Second, bring the eternal light and love that you are into this physical experience; play and create and have fun as the dolphins have reminded you to do. Your lives are meant to be so very good for you. You are so much more powerful than you know yourself to be. Start perceiving yourself beyond the limitations that have so far defined you.

For the first time, you are coming into levels of consciousness and frequency and vibration where you are accessing potentials and possibilities beyond anything that has ever been conceived of before.

You live in a beautiful, loving, harmonious, abundant world that is now beaming with an entirely new energy and level of consciousness where you can experience what many refer to as Heaven on Earth. Moreover, you have the great pleasure of creating it any way you wish it to be.

Your vision is powerful, and you are ready—a creator within your own creation. As you live your life to the fullest, intentionally choosing the experiences you want to have, you'll begin to realize your oneness with Source and with all things. And in your awakening, you will seed human consciousness and expand the potentials and possibilities for your entire human family. Although your brain will never understand this, your self-realization will lead to the expansion of consciousness here and in dimensions far beyond.

From this perspective, it is accurate to say that you are God's greatest creation. And because you are Source, you are also that which you call God. You are creator within your own creation.

So have some fun. Go play, create, and discover. Go enjoy it all.

SECTION 5

GOD

In this section, The Council discusses our inevitable realization of the divinity inherently within us all, and offers guidance for nourishing this relationship so that we may live lives of unimaginable joy.

We are pleased and delighted to have the opportunity to speak with you once again, our dear and wonderful friend. We remind you to open to and allow the incredible Source energy that is here for you. It is in the opening and the allowing that you tune in to the incredible power within you that is always available. When your human mind feels overwhelmed by all there is to do—because in the doing there is always more and more to be done—tune in to that state of being where all things are done through you. Go within and tune in to Source energy; open to it and allow it to flow fully through you. That is when you will move incredible and miraculous things into physical form that are beyond your wildest dreams.

Remember, it is all energy. And consciousness moves energy into form. So as you move yourself into higher levels of consciousness, you will move energy into form aligned with the highest perspectives and potentials for the most magical and miraculous unfolding.

Where would you like to begin, our friend?

It's great to be with you again, Council. This chapter is about God. You've said that the human mind will not be able to fathom some things. But would you attempt to explain God to us, and how we may come to know the Divine?

Indeed. We'd like to remind you that when you label anything, you begin to limit it and all the potential and possibility within it. Yet we understand how the human mind works. Most all your experience is perceived through the filter of your physical senses: you believe what you hear, see, taste, touch, smell, and think about. And these experiences are stored in your mind. Your brain is a collection of accumulated data and information. And it will always be making associations, looking for proof, and formulating explanations. This is a natural aspect of the human mind; it's looking for similarities, and it's looking for something that associates with whatever you perceive or believe about your experience.

At times, you can feel a greater presence focused upon you or a greater presence flowing through you; you can feel the presence of what you might call the Divine. But many humans would say they have no proof of this thing called God, as interpreted by their physical senses and perceived by their mind.

When you're trying to understand something through the limited perspective of the human lens, it's easy to see how the concept of God can become skewed. How can you accurately interpret something that cannot be perceived with the physical senses? Therefore, for many, God is just a concept or a misunderstanding.

Primitive humans had no way of perceiving Source energy, or God consciousness, let alone talking about it or perceiving themselves as vessels for Source energy. While they may have witnessed what you call supernatural things, they couldn't interpret these events through the concept of a God.

As humans evolved, you came into more communal ways of living—forming tribes and villages. Oftentimes, the leader of the tribe would be a man, and he would seem to have all the power. As such, you began conceptualizing this thing called God, and God became an anthropomorphic sort of force or power. In those times, all that humans knew was that men seemed to possess the power and authority, so God was created in the image of man.

Over time, the concept of God became a man with all the power, sitting on a cloud, judging humans for what you had done right or wrong, good or bad, and whether—through your thoughts and deeds and actions—you were sinning and displeasing Him, or praising and pleasing Him. Furthermore, if you did what the man on the cloud expected you to do, you got into Heaven; if you didn't, you went to Hell.

As we said previously, God does not have a personality. God is pure Source energy. God is light. God is love. God is vibration. God is frequency. God is the power that can do anything. God is the power that can do the impossible. God is pure Source energy expressing itself in the world. But it does not have a personality and certainly is not judging you.

Now, as we've also said, Source energy is always responding to you. You are either allowing more Source energy, God consciousness, infinite power in your life, or you're limiting it. The more you allow it to flow through you, the more you will feel and experience the presence of God within.

How you experience God will always be determined by your level of consciousness and, therefore, how much you are experiencing the presence of God, the Divine in your life. You're the one that gives the meaning.

There is no force outside of you creating your Heaven or Hell; it's you. You are creating it based on the level of consciousness that you are bringing to your life experiences and the amount of Source energy you're allowing through in any moment. Nevertheless, when anyone releases the density of the body, they reemerge back into Source energy—the Source energy of the God that they are and the Source energy of All That Is.

Could someone be very happy, grateful, feel blessed, and experience Heaven on Earth without having any awareness of their level of consciousness or vibration? Yes. They're just naturally allowing more Source energy; they're allowing God consciousness into their heart.

Many have struggled with interpreting the Bible. How could the word of God be interpreted in so many ways? Today, even, you're in a very different place in your own evolution of consciousness. If you pause and tune in to the highest guidance on some of your questions, just like we're doing here, your understanding would be very different than when the Bible was written a thousand years ago. And we're not just speaking about the Bible; we are talking about any religious text. Indeed, humanity's consciousness is rising.

From our perspective, religion and God (or the concept of God) are two very different things. Religion is manmade. God is eternal and ever-present, and you're either allowing God consciousness or you're denying it. God is Source energy. God is the infinite power. God is the divine love that you are and that everyone and everything is too. God is the Source energy that flows through everything.

Yet so many struggle with the concept of accepting that they are that which you call God, yet if you were to ask us, "What is God?" we would say God is you. You are expressing as the Source energy you call God.

Beautiful. Please expand on this.

The idea that Source energy doesn't have a personality is very difficult for humans to understand because you have personalities. And we celebrate your magnificent personalities; they are part of your amazing creations. Although Source energy, Creator energy, God consciousness can create a personality, it is not a personality; it's an energy. And some would say it doesn't make sense to surrender to energy, to something that doesn't have an intelligence. Yet we would say, "Oh, but it does have intelligence."

That intelligence is evident in human form, and far beyond that as a multidimensional being. As we said earlier, this intelligence guides every aspect of your development, from an embryo into a fetus into a baby and into an adult, perfectly designed for your environment to live in joy. Throughout all stages of development, you draw to you—through the intelligence that is you—all that you need to survive and thrive. That intelligence is always guiding your life.

There is a highest good in all situations. Your consciousness combined with that Source energy is what many are really referring to when they're referring to God.

That makes sense, though it's almost impossible for me to grasp how any of us even got here, how and when reality began. How could we even be having this conversation? I know that

my questioning implies a timeline, and we've talked about time being an illusion. But even listening to you now and contemplating that we're here—that I have a body and a mind, and I am living on this beautiful planet and speaking to you right now—how? How could any of this be happening, even if it's all an illusion?

In terms of what's most important, your question of origin matters far less than the thoughts you are thinking and the level of consciousness that you are embodying, right now.

You are here in physical form, aware of higher levels of consciousness and aware of the Source energy that is you and is within you. Grasping this is enough. With this awareness, you can now tune in to these higher levels of consciousness while opening to and allowing Source energy to flow through you and create in physical form. It is so much more important for you to be right here, right now because anything and everything is possible for you only in this now moment.

You have limitless potentials and infinite possibilities. And you are here at the most important time in any lifetime in human history. You are here for the greatest transformation of consciousness that has ever occurred on your planet. And every thought that you think really does matter, because as you well know, our friend, thoughts become things.

So it is very important for you to understand the power you have within this force field of consciousness that is you. You are a force field of consciousness made up of particles of infinite creation that are always responding to you—God particles, if you will. Just understand this. And with it, the most important thing you can do is to create your life the way you want it to be and live it to the fullest. Express the God consciousness that you are in everything that you do.

Perceive and move yourself into an awareness that you are much more than this physical body and much more than the physical senses can perceive. The more you elevate your consciousness into these realms of infinite possibility and sense beyond the limitations in the human experience, the more you will experience your God consciousness. And the more you experience your God consciousness, the more potentials and possibilities become available to you.

So, in understanding our presence here—in terms of *who is God*—we are God's wish come alive, to self-reflect, self-realize, and to then carry the baton forward into further realms with our own creativity? Does that capture it?

If you wish; that would be perfect.

Is there any other angle or twist other than God simply wanted to exist in form, as me, Sara, and everyone else, just for the joy of playing and creating and enjoying this adventure?

There is a reason for you choosing to focus your consciousness into physical form on the planet currently. However, we aren't here to tell you that there's something you're supposed to do or that you should be doing. Again, you're not here to fix a broken world or to save humanity from anything.

Having said this, there is an incredible opportunity for an entire species to transform their consciousness and access potentials and possibilities you, God, have never explored before. You have all chosen to focus yourself into this human experience to be the ones who remember the vision or the dream for that and then create it.

Yes. Understanding God through self-realization and realizing the divinity within ourselves. I'm looking forward to talking about exactly that: enlightenment, ascension, and ascended masters. Before that, could you first explain the power of prayer? And what is the best way to pray as a stepping stone toward the transformation of our own consciousness?

Simply said, prayer allows you to focus Source energy into your intentions. When you pray, you are focusing on what it is you want to create or manifest or experience in physical form, which is a wonderful thing. And there can be relief in the voicing of your desires. Prayers are a form of focusing particles of infinite creation on intended outcomes. However, many of you pray from a place of lack or separation: you pray to some force or thing outside of you, believing that you don't have the power. Instead, understand that you are the power, that the power is available to you, and that you are a critical part of the creative process.

We spoke earlier about how you continually re-create your experiences through repetitive thoughts, beliefs, visions, perceptions, actions, awareness, and emotional habits. However, as you move beyond these patterns, and begin living in the expansion, you will create new things. Most of you don't realize that there is a clean slate and fresh start available to you every moment of every day.

Instead of engaging the energy of hoping, begging, or wishing for something outside of you to answer your prayers, it would be far more empowering for you to live the manifestation of those prayers right now. The way to do this is to tune in; go into the consciousness within you and feel into the formless realities in the higher levels of consciousness where anything and everything is possible. Truly feel the manifestation right here, right now of that which you want to be experiencing. See it and feel it and experience it in your physical body as your reality now. This is so much more powerful.

You can use the activity of prayer to tune in, to open to and connect with Source energy, and then to feel and allow that Source energy into your life. When you connect your hands to pray and bow your head, you are honoring your connection to your Source energy—the power within you that is always available to you—and to the higher levels of consciousness that always know the highest and best good for all. Your soul, your higher self, is that higher level of consciousness that is always connected to Source, God, the Divine. When you make that connection, and you really tune in, and you can feel your prayer as already done, created, and manifested, then your prayer is already answered.

What often happens after that, however, is that you then let go of that connection. You go back to perceiving the situation through your limited human senses and think that your prayer was not answered. You can get discouraged and distracted from your higher-level creations; you lose faith.

Envisioning, meditating, prayer, gratitude, appreciation—anything where you are tuning into and perceiving the Source energy that is you and is within you and always available to you—can be incredibly helpful for you on your journey through consciousness. These actions will expand the potentials and possibilities within your experience, making the miracles you are praying for even more possible.

THE ASCENDED MASTER STATE

And this envisioning, seeing it as already done, would also apply to the ethereal aspects we might desire–of being wiser, feeling more love, knowing we're provided for, connecting with Source energy, for example. If we can imagine that if we are *already* self-realized, we could undoubtedly advance more quickly into higher levels of consciousness, like those of ascended masters?

Indeed. So, as a reminder, the higher realms are not hierarchically better. However, beings in these levels of consciousness do not believe the illusions you believe in. When you believe that you are lacking, and you believe you are your limitations, and you believe you're separate from Source energy—and anything and everything that is available to you—you will be in fear and separation. These are your illusions. And from your limited human perspective, you think the only thing that's going to fix that and make that better is to go out and try to force and effort and make things happen. Usually, this just results in more frustration and more resistance and more experiences of lack or limitation. While the higher realms know that's not who they really are or what's really going on here.

This is why we say there is no judgment from our side, ever. We are never judging you, your soul is never judging you, and Source is never judging you. Yet the moment you tune in to the higher levels and start allowing for inspiration and opening to and allowing the energy and the light to guide the way for you, suddenly new opportunities, new potentials, new pathways begin to unfold.

Remember, these levels of consciousness are not outside of you. However, if you think you are only human, and your human thinks it knows what's going on and what's right for you and all you need—you are limiting yourself. That's not your human's job.

To allow a grander perspective and to allow a higher view, allow the Divine to unfold perfectly in your life. It's the part of you in higher realms of consciousness that sees the whole picture. None of which is separate from you unless you hold yourself apart from it.

And I can only access that if my own perceptions, beliefs, and desires–to be in that high realm, to see the complete picture–support it. And I would say, and I'm sure many of our readers would agree, that we are now at a place where we realize everything is of God, by God, pure God–that we are absolutely, totally God. In this place, I am completely fearless about death because I know I'm an eternal being. And from this higher perspective, I can sincerely say that I don't think of myself anymore as only human, encased in flesh, just reacting to the

world that's whirling around me, supposedly of its own volition. I do think that I, and many of our readers, have reached this point. Yet I feel that there's more for me to comprehend or, perhaps, assimilate and integrate. Maybe on some level I don't really believe what I just said, because I still act very human and at times do not see things from that higher perspective. It seems, still, that there is something between me and that ascended master state.

Your ascended master self has gone into higher levels of consciousness or awareness; it has ascended into awareness of realms beyond the physical.

A master of oneself is simply someone who is at the top of his or her game; they have come into a level of mastery, into a level of excellence. Mastering the Self, the God part of you, the higher self, the eternal-being part of you—that's what an ascended master is.

You do not realize that at all times you are simultaneously moving toward mastery of higher realms and living as the God force that you are. All of you are. You're also embracing this human experience, bringing higher perspectives into physical form. That is what an ascended master here on Earth does.

You know all of this; we know you do. The reason why we continuously remind you to open and allow is because we want you to let it be easy and effortless. And your human would say, "But I have timelines. I have deadlines. I have things that need to get done. I run a company. I have customers. I have services to perform. I have events on these dates. I have things I've got to get done. I've got financial responsibilities. I've got responsibilities for my family. I have all these things that my human must get done."

From our perspective, it's really quite simple: *you're just perceiving your stories more than you're perceiving higher levels of consciousness.* The more you perceive from higher dimensions, the more you will live in the complete and total flow of all things, and their perfect unfolding in the divine right time, trusting and knowing that it will likely turn out even better than what your human could have figured out or done.

We understand that there's a balance between flow and important obligations, such as picking up your daughter at a certain time. And yet even then, you may be holding yourself in a belief of lack or limitation. For example, you might say, "If I don't pick her up at the right time, she won't be safe," or "I'm a bad parent if I'm not on time." Many people end up rushing around to do certain things at certain times because of their stories.

As we said earlier, it's the level of consciousness that you're in when they're doing these things that's most important. You could be really flowing in the unfolding, just like anything else, or it could be stressful. How you do these things is always of your choosing.

There are things you want to do in the human experience that you believe need to be done within specific time frames and deadlines. And it is perfect; we understand that this is part of the experience. We just want you to do everything, as much as possible, from the highest level of consciousness. When you ask about enlightenment, or the ascended master state, that is how we would describe it for the human experience. It is allowing yourself into the highest vibration and the higher state of consciousness *all the time in everything that you do.*

The ascended master state is understanding that you are here on Earth because of your incredible love for existence, humanity, the planet, and the animals, choosing to possess a continued focus from both physical and nonphysical realms to guide it all forward at this incredible time.

WAYSHOWERS AND REALIZED MASTERS

So, who are and were the enlightened masters of Earth? And did Jesus, Buddha, and likely many others achieve precisely what you just outlined? Then, as part of their evolving mission, they became wayshowers? Could you clarify this?

There are many enlightened masters that you don't know by name. And there is certainly no threshold or limitation for anyone who comes into a moment of what you would call enlightenment. In other words, in any moment a person feels and experiences and understands themself as the Divine in physical form, they are considered enlightened. In fact, you all came from an enlightened master state, from which you focused yourself into physical form.

Indeed, there are beings who choose to come into the human experience to be wayshowers or leaders or to light the path for others. But all of them came into their own realization first, and then they allowed the energy and the light to guide their various roles. And once they were realized, in the state of allowing Source energy, living in higher levels of consciousness, they were considered enlightened beings in physical form.

All of you choose different experiences in physical form at different times, related to the evolution of your soul and its progression through consciousness. And, indeed, you have many enlightened beings, or ascended masters, on your planet currently.

And there's no reason why anyone reading this book can't choose that path for themselves, if it's what they feel called, inspired, or guided to do.

Again, many enlightened masters, in the past, came into realization and then chose to leave the physical incarnation almost immediately. Things are different now. We tell you that this is the time for embodying the enlightened master that you are, staying in physical form, and creating your life the way you want it to be, living your life to the fullest and living your highest potential. This is the most important thing you can do to serve at this time. Live fully. Love fully. Be all that you are.

Would you go so far to say that enlightenment, as you've described it, is every human's goal?

Indeed. We refer to it as realization, which is coming into the realization of the truth of who you are and integrating every part of you. Realization is the intention of every soul's journey in physical form.

When you access that Source energy, that infinite power that you are, then you live in such a flow with life that you don't need or want *for anything,* because you know you're connected to everything. As you get into higher realms, everything is available to you. At these levels, you are playing and creating and manifesting in the realm of infinite potentials and possibilities. It's all there for you.

The same is true here in physical form. Moving from formless into form takes a bit longer sometimes, but it doesn't mean that you can't access the full manifestation of it here and now.

Once everyone's enlightened, if that day comes, will there still be adventure, or will that be game over?

Oh, indeed, there will be adventure. And in many ways, once everyone is enlightened, *it will just be the beginning.*

Our desire is to bring forth this vibration, this wisdom, this light, and this love to you in a way that all who are ready to receive it can do so. And as each of you begin to perceive beyond your human, you'll likewise begin to have experiences that are beyond anything you have yet imagined.

But everything within the human experience today—all the potentials and the possibilities—have come because of your desires, intentions, wants, and a whole lot of asking within lower dimensions of consciousness. Now you are beginning to experience the full-blown manifestation and creation of them in this dimension of physical form. And the amazing thing is that you are one of these manifestations.

We speak of the New Earth as a place where there is peace, joy, love, harmony, abundance, well-being, and freedom for all. It is here for your choosing now, and you are choosing it every time you elevate yourself beyond lack, limitation, fear, and separation. And *everyone* in the New Earth experience with you will also be experiencing that peace, joy, love, harmony, abundance, well-being and freedom as you play, co-create, have fun, love and interact. However, you don't all choose the same things; and not everyone needs to be choosing the New Earth for others to be living in it.

All that's needed is for you to embrace yourself as creator of your own creation and embrace all others as creators within their own creations, respecting their right to choose for themselves. Then you all just expand the potentials and possibilities from there.

Is this what you were saying is meant by the Second Coming of Christ and the gradual awakening of civilization?

Well, it's not going to be gradual at all from here on out. While the last thousands of years may have been gradual, the awakening of humanity is upon you now and is happening at an accelerated rate. The Second Coming of Christ is realization; it is your realization of the Christ consciousness within you, the God within you, the Source within you, the Divine, the infinite power within you, whatever you feel most comfortable calling it. The ascended master being that you know as Jesus came to Earth at a time when the consciousness on the planet was very different than what it is now. He came into realization or enlightenment and then ascended within physical form into higher levels of consciousness, where he accessed more and more Source energy, which allowed him to create amazing manifestations in physical form.

At that time, very few on the planet had ever accessed that level of consciousness. Today, your collective human consciousness is at a much higher vibration, and your individual human consciousnesses—for those of you who have been awakening and are awakened—are much, much, much higher. So, you are naturally, because of your vibration and your level of consciousness, coming into that same state of awareness and enlightenment that Jesus had. The Second Coming of Christ is here, and it is your opportunity to come into Christ consciousness within yourself.

INNER AWAKENING AND YOUR GUIDING LIGHT

How much of this awakening within each person is dependent upon latent psychic, physical, or metaphysical attributes or abilities that we've earned in this or other lifetimes? Does anyone who wants to become realized already have all the equipment they need? Do we have to be especially gifted, or is it just a matter of believing that we can realize and then raising our vibration to match the belief?

All of you have the equipment you need. However, you are unique extensions of Source energy with different passions having progressed to varying degrees due to different experiences. Nothing else matters. You will naturally find yourself drawn to unique expressions of yourself at various times of your life, including your resonance with truth and realization.

That's why we say, follow the energy and let the light guide the way. Come into the moment. The energy will always guide you to everything you need—to the people you need, to the resources you need, and to the experiences you need. Everything is always happening for you—for your highest good. Open to and allow the energy, and remember, it's not outside of you, it is within you, it is you. It's the aspect of you that can see beyond the lack, limitation, fear, separation, and illusion. All you need to do is tap into that.

What might we do to become more aware of the light that's guiding us? Might we literally set an alarm for various times throughout our day and, when it goes off, tune in and ask, "How do I feel?" or "What would I like to do?" That's my latest technique.

Indeed. However, we would suggest that you ask *what brings you joy*. So, when you tune in, ask, "What could I do right now that would bring me joy?" Or simply tune in to the feeling of joy.

For many, that's more elusive than it may seem. How do we shift our focus toward more joy?

The first question we ask anyone who is in a reality that they don't want to be in is, "What do you want?" Let's say that instead of your many tasks, you would rather be experiencing a reality of freedom, creativity, abundance, and flow.

When we say you are creator within your own creation, that means you can create your life the way you want it to be. So, if you want an experience of life where everything feels in the flow, and you feel a sense of freedom and abundance like never before, and to experience your days as fun and joyful and effortless, then choose to open and allow that energy. And with your focus and attention on those energies, allow the next perfect step to come to you; allow the next inspired action to come to you.

Here's an example of what this might look like. Let's say that you have some business responsibilities that you want to get done today, but you also want to go for a run, have some quiet time for yourself, and some quality time with your family. Most of these items won't have to be done at a specific time, but for any that do, put them into your calendar. Then, with this awareness, and considering what is left on your list, as you begin your day, ask, "What on this list could I do that would bring me joy?" Then see what lights up and go do that thing. And, when that thing is done, go back and choose again, by asking the same question. And as you're doing these things, instead of thinking of what's next, and all that you've got to get done today, enjoy what you are doing: stay present, stay tuned in, stay aware so you can notice how the energy is flowing. If the energy stops flowing, then stop and see where the energy and the light is guiding you. Creating more joy is a continuous process of tuning in to where the energy and light is guiding you and choosing that.

If the energy starts guiding you in a different direction, to a different task, while you haven't finished the current task, and you start thinking, "I have to finish this task before I move on," and you start pushing and forcing energy because of some rule you have that once you start something you have to finish it, you are now out of the flow. And you start rushing and feeling agitated because the energy and light guided you in another direction, but this task "has to be done first; if I don't get something completely done, I'm not going to feel good about myself." That's your human.

So, then you think to yourself, "Well, I can't trust that inspiration because it's pulling me in another direction, but I've got to get this one thing done right now." Is that true? Sometimes, but many times you're just telling the same story you've told yourself many times before because following the energy and the light feels uncomfortable to your human. So you're not opening to and allowing what it is that you really want, which is why you're not feeling the joy.

So it's as simple as practice, practice, practice?

It's even more perception and awareness. In every moment, if you're perceiving from the grandest perspective of who you really are and what's really going on here, then you can stay present and conscious and expand the force field of consciousness that is you, which will attract everything you need to stay in the flow of your desires, which in this example are freedom, creativity, and abundance.

Is that a practice? Yes, but it's not as much of a practice as it is you stepping fully into being creator within your own creation. Once you take full responsibility for being creator within your own creation and for creating your life the way you want it to be, you are at a level of consciousness where it is simply choiceless to follow the energy and let the light guide the way toward the things that you want to be experiencing more of—more flow, more freedom, more abundance, more fun, more joy. You will no longer want to push and force energy where you think it should go, because you will understand that when you do that you are bringing more of that into your reality.

Remember, as a force field of consciousness made up of particles of infinite creation that are always responding to you, *reality is moving through you*. You'll know when you're not open to and allowing the energy and light by how you feel. If you're feeling anxious and uptight and edgy, that is the reality you are moving into physical form. On the other hand, if you are feeling happy and peaceful and joyful, that is the reality that you are moving into form.

Just like the analogy of a director with the camera filming a scene. All you see in the theater is what they focused on. The same is true for you. You have unlimited potential and infinite possibilities. What you are focused on is creating your reality. So if you really are focused on coming into the realization of yourself as an enlightened master and that's what you're focused on, then it is about drawing that reality through you.

What about stories of spontaneous illumination, a sudden and permanent awakening or realization? Does everybody have some form of spontaneous enlightenment, or is it always gradual? Is spontaneous illumination even a reasonable pursuit? Or is it always based on the prior inner work done by the individual?

Most people actually do have spontaneous illumination experiences; this is not rare. Where in one moment there is a question or confusion, and in the next there's understanding and awareness. Some of these experiences can indeed be profound, and many are fleeting.

What you choose to do with these experiences is what matters. There are many who have an experience of this kind and want to feel it again; they want to know what it was, understand it, continue to be aware of it, and connect with it again. So their focus upon it will continue to draw them into its vibration, into a consciousness where they can experience more of that. And as they perceive and experience more of that, they will begin to perceive even greater potentials and possibilities for themself and an even grander perspective of who they are. Which leads to even greater expansion.

On the other hand, someone else could have a similar experience of perceiving themself beyond their limitation but then go right back to the illusion, doubting or denying that it ever happened.

There are also many stories in your various traditions of those who have achieved enlightenment or God consciousness. The settings range from traveling into the desert or forest, to the top of a mountain; maybe they went off for 40 days and 40 nights. These are often stories of a person leaving behind circumstances that were reflecting limitation so that they could perceive themselves beyond them.

In that desire to experience themself as something beyond who they knew themself to be, they were able to reach a level of consciousness and a level of vibration where that became their new way of being.

Very few of you right now believe you can go into the desert or the forest or the mountains for 40 days—or some other significant period of time—to contemplate yourself beyond lack and limitation and move your awareness into higher levels of consciousness. So, instead, you must do it while living in your modern world.

This may seem a bit tricky, because when you're in the exact same environment day after day, feeling and thinking and seeing and tasting and touching and smelling all the same things, it doesn't seem like much is really changing. But you are always creating and re-creating.

Part of the reason you enjoy vacations and traveling to new places so much is because you leave your familiar environment and go into the new. Thus, you may perceive yourself very differently when you travel, because you are experiencing yourself beyond much of the lack and limitation of your normal routines.

While having a spontaneous awakening might be easier when you are in new experiences, it can happen at any time. It is then, as we've said, of your choosing what to do with it. For some, the experience is so strong they must find their way back—no matter what they have to do or how long it might take. Once someone has an awakening, their ascension into higher levels of consciousness can happen very quickly. However, sometimes those changes happen over much longer periods of time, say many years. It all depends on how a person re-creates themself once they have the awareness that they are much more than they believed themself to be.

I think we call these transcendental experiences. This might sound trite, but how do we manifest some of these? What are they a product of—intention, expectation, contemplation?

Indeed, you create these experiences through awareness and perception. As we've said, what you are focusing on and the meaning you're giving it is what's creating your reality. So, if you desire to experience yourself as God, as Source energy, as the Divine, or experience higher power—your infinite power—you only need to be aware of it and then perceive yourself into it and beyond. Some use tools or techniques, such as breathwork, meditation, or music, to get into a transcended state, but once they are there, they give it meaning, which is what creates what happens next. Does that make sense?

Very much. What powers and abilities does someone who is fully self-realized have? Could they override physical laws? I've heard of the ability to ascend and take the body into much higher vibrations and disappear or, perhaps, bilocate–be in more than one physical location at the same time. Could we lift heavy blocks and monolithic stones and travel through wormholes? What's possible?

They could align themself into a state of peace, joy, freedom, abundance, love, and well-being, beyond their wildest dreams. At any time, no matter what was going on around them.

Anything is possible as you tune in to all sorts of dimensions and activities, including telepathy and teleportation. That is the power that you would access, and that is the power that, as you say, moves mountains. But these experiences still wouldn't compare to the realization of that which has been most desired by the human experience for centuries—peace, joy, freedom, love, abundance, well-being, and harmony *within yourself.* All of which can be achieved for humanity, once you create it for yourself.

That's so good.
I deeply want to bring myself to a clearer understanding of God, being God, awakening the god inside of me, and possessing Christ consciousness to live these ideas.

I have a sense that I can perhaps use a bit of contemplative thought to get to that place of release and allowance, from which I should be able to let go and not have to figure any more out. But it seems rather difficult to bring myself, my consciousness, to this point of receivership.

It comes back to really allowing energy to serve you. And that is what is meant by being in the flow. It's such an overused word. You think you're in the flow when you're getting everything done, it's easy, and you have a green light, or when you find a parking spot. It's so much more than that.

It is really allowing energy, without an agenda, to guide you. And if you could just start opening to this in little moments throughout your day, the little moments will be more moments, and the more moments will be bigger, longer moments. Then you'll realize you are living fully enlightened, the true realized master that you are, following, opening, and allowing energy to serve you. Allowing more of what you are, which is energy and light.

Your life in the flow and your life fully allowing energy to serve you, allowing energy to light the way, might start looking differently in your day-to-day life, but you don't have to start there. Start with little moments, easy moments. Then let them be more. You might find that even within what you do and your service to the world that you *are* totally in the flow in all of it and you don't have such a rigorous schedule of "I only do this from this time to this time," because the energy might not be there in that time.

It sounds so simple, and I know it is so simple. What should I do, though? Is there a technique? Is meditation the key?

That is where you deny yourself. What should I do? Should I be meditating because I'm not doing this right? Should I be meditating because I'm not there yet? Should I be meditating because I'm not as enlightened as I should be? That is denying and limiting yourself.

Is it a correct perception that as I'm more in truth or, as you phrased it, surrendering to the flow, allowing and following the energy, I will raise my vibration? Meaning I'm then more able to engage the elements to do my bidding? That the whole equation is one of raising my vibration, being more in tune, more of a believer, less of a denier, to the point where I can speak and the elements will respond immediately; seeds will grow into trees, flowers will bloom, winds will gust, and seas will calm. Is that a proper view of the task before me? To raise my vibe and summon the energy so that I can not only manipulate the elements but receive and feel ecstasy, know divine love, and go anywhere I can imagine?

This is going to help you a lot. We're going to give you a completely different perspective here on what you are asking, because all of what you are asking is still needing to change your conditions and external circumstances for you to find the power, peace, love, beauty, joy, and fulfillment *within* you. You're still trying to manipulate and control the elements around you in order to achieve the creation that can only be found and created within you. Once you create the vibrational resonance within you, all the particles of matter within the force field around you begin to reorganize themselves to align with you.

Again, and this is important. You're trying to change external circumstances with your force and might. You're trying from needing and wanting something outside of you to be different. You're trying to take on the task of manipulating and controlling the elements versus understanding what is really meant by *you are God*; you are creator within your own creation. God created all of this beauty and then stepped into the experience and the expansion of creation. It comes only from within you and then expands in the force field around you.

You're still trying to make this a lot of work. You're still trying to force and control particles instead of getting into alignment with the power that you have, knowing that the particles around you will reorganize themselves to align with the frequency you are in. It is the Law of Resonance. You are the strongest vibration. You are consciousness in human form. You are the highest frequency because you are allowing for consciousness from a place of knowing yourself as consciousness.

Consciousness is not thought, and consciousness is not thinking. It's not the mental mind. You cannot mentally feel. You can't go through the mind to feel. Your mind interprets the feeling. It is about your consciousness moving you into a vibration, and because you are creator within your own creation, you draw to you from the force field around you the particles that are in alignment with that. Just your focus on a particular alignment will draw the particles to reorganize and align themselves to harmonize with you.

Come into full and total alignment with peace within you—because you are peace. Peace is what you are. You only get more of what you are, not what you want. You don't get smooth waters because you want them, nor by commanding the waves to cease. You get more of what you are.

Here's one step before it, dear master. Let's say you are trying to fly a kite with your daughter in little wind. If you are really following energy, you might get guided to do something else in that moment that is more aligned to the energy. And then, 20 minutes later, all of a sudden the energy goes all into flying your kite and here comes the wind.

You have far greater senses within your field of consciousness than you allow because you're still trying to force a particular agenda when and how you think it should be.

Now, will you get to the state that you are desirous of? We assure you, you will. But there's a step before it, which is coming into impeccable creation, mastering impeccable creation, which is when you're not trying to manipulate everything out there because you know it is created from within you and extended and expanded from you into the field around you.

Yes, I see and feel this, and it's really helpful. The assignment, the challenge, the adventure before me, then, is more fully integrating the truth of my total divinity in every moment, which will be part and parcel of following the energy. I don't want to be a manifester of winds because I happen to pick the right times when it's gusty. I want to have such mastery that if there's no wind and I want wind, I can have wind!

And you shall have it. But there's a step in between: elevating your awareness, consciousness, and frequency into a place where all of this is possible for you. The more you try to push it, the more doubt you're going to create, which is just going to delay the very creation that you would like to experience within your own life.

You said something earlier: to step up and align with the energy of who you really are. I feel like that's what's before me.

Yes. And it is elevating your state of consciousness, moving you into elevated states of consciousness.

But what is an elevated state of consciousness?

Remember, the 3rd Dimension of consciousness is an experience of separation, not knowing who you are, in a density where you are not allowing a whole lot of energy and therefore experiencing a lower vibration. In the 3rd Dimension of consciousness, where there is separation, there is lack, there is prejudice, there is not enoughness, there is you not being good enough. And in that, because of the slower rate of frequency within a more dense state of consciousness, you learn that the only way to get things done is to control, manipulate, force, effort, take massive action, and exhaust yourself.

There is fear and there is suffering within that level of consciousness. As you begin to raise your vibration, you step into a higher state of consciousness where you realize you are more than your circumstances, you are more than your lack of money, you are more than the limitation you believe yourself to be. This next state of consciousness is the 4th Dimension.

This is a dimension of consciousness where you're still trying to fix yourself, you're trying to heal yourself, you're trying to manifest things and change your circumstances. There's always a focus on healing and releasing and working on yourself, and it's a wonderful thing, but you are now stepping into even more. People get stuck in that dimension of consciousness because they continually perceive themselves not complete, whole, or worthy enough yet. They still judge themselves.

And then, you step into the 5th Dimension of pure love. There's a new energy here. There's a new level of consciousness here, which means that the laws work differently, they really do. Force and effort will always entangle you with lower dimensions of consciousness. Judgment of yourself and others will always move you out of the 5th Dimension.

Now, apply what we said earlier. The 5th Dimension is a state of pure love, ease, effortlessness, harmony, opening and allowing energy, pure light, pure joy, knowing yourself as the God that you are, living within your own experience of Heaven on Earth where you get more of all that you are and life continues to expand. Expanding peace, fulfillment, harmony, well-being, and you begin to step into the infinite intelligence that you are. In the 5th Dimension, your well-being and your abundance are assured.

The allowing of that continues to raise your frequency. You begin to move into impeccable creation or True Creation, which is much different than what you experience when using force, effort, or manifestation from a place of lack and limitation.

You can absolutely have everything that you want, but you don't have to go down into lack and limitation to create more of what you are. You're still wanting to entangle with lack and limitation—I need, I want—in order to create, which will always move you down into lower dimensions of consciousness, where those things that you want to create and experience are separate from you. Does that make sense to you?

So, from where I'm at right now, creating this shift is simply a matter of elevating my consciousness, and to elevate my consciousness it's about identifying and feeling where the energy is.

Do you know why you want to be and do all of the things you want? Do you know why you want those things? You want to be able to fly a kite, create the wind, calm the seas because you're wanting to prove to yourself that you are God, that you are Creator? It is because you still doubt it and you don't know it yet, which is why you're not fully experiencing yourself as it. Let go of your doubt and your need to prove it to yourself in order to know yourself as the God that you are.

The human part of you is trying to force yourself into an experience, which will happen, we promise you, we assure you. We could almost give you the exact timing of it, although much is still based on your own free will. You will attain absolute knowing in a very short period of time within this lifetime, we assure you. This is the life that you incarnated for your enlightenment and realization and then to stay on the planet in physical form as the realized ascended master that you are. The more you are at peace with that, you will feel and know "I am the peace. I am the light. I am the truth."

You're still trying to do tricks and prove to yourself that you can perform magic. There's no need to prove to yourself or anyone that you are creator within your own creation. Allow yourself into the I Am Creator frequency.

Well, the reason for the tricks is that I feel like I know I am God to my core. Yet, as I shared it doesn't seem I'm as effective in expressing and living that as I'd like. And I think a quick telltale sign if I'm there or not is if I can calm the seas or gust up some wind.

—

It's not that I care about interrupting the sea or making wind, I don't, and I don't intend to be ostentatious about it . . . but you're right. They're tests of mine because I'm still not in a state of ecstasy and all-knowingness.

You can focus yourself into any reality you choose. If ecstasy is what you want, it would take a very short period of time for you to focus yourself into ecstasy and feel every cell in your body aligned to a vibration of ecstasy. You could go into your heart and begin to feel ecstasy, really feel ecstasy within you. Then direct every cell of your body to align with the vibration of ecstasy until you feel every cell of your body is in ecstasy. Feel ecstasy in every cell of your body from the top of your head to the bottom of your feet and out your fingertips. You have aligned and focused every single cell of your body into a frequency of ecstasy. You have focused every cell of your body into a vibration of knowing from the top of your head to the bottom of your feet, out your fingertips in every direction in this entire force field of existence that is you, which expands as high as you can see and as far as you can go, deep beneath you into the Earth. You are focusing every cell and every particle in your force field into an alignment of all knowing. At that point, the seas would be calm and you could create any reality you choose.

Instead, align with that which is the reality you want to create by first focusing yourself into any reality that you choose.

That is very different than wanting to force and change your external elements to be the way you think they should be when you're still not in the vibration of the reality you want to create.

We understand you want to get into an expanded, creational field. You want to get into your force field of creation. So, when you wake up in the morning or throughout your day, ask yourself, "What do I want to feel? What do I choose? What do I want more of?" If it is ecstasy, then take a few moments to focus yourself and every cell of your body into ecstasy until you feel that ecstasy within you and all around you as far as you can see until you feel your light shining brightly. Then, within that light infuse every particle with the frequency of ecstasy or peace or harmony or abundance or prosperity or freedom or all-knowingness. That is how you draw to you experiences that are aligned to your creation. You draw the particles to you in your field, which means you're not chasing after external circumstances trying to make them happen.

You are particles of infinite creation. That's what you are. That's what your cells are. This is the most powerful creation that you have. When you begin to step into knowing that you are one with All That Is. You have learned to powerfully focus your own particles, and then you can move into the world around you, understanding your oneness with All That Is, and you begin to experience the waves within your own creation. There are no waves out there. It is all an extension of you. And then you expand the particles of creation that you are into the waves. And as you focus yourself into peace, the particles of the waves begin to smooth out and move into a resonance with the peace that you are.

And by the way, relationships begin to look very different too. You no longer try to negotiate what you want from a human level, in a dimension of lower consciousness and lower frequency. Your relationships will be more peaceful, harmonious, and loving. All relationships are a reflection of your relationship to Source and reflect your own level of consciousness.

You are consciousness. Your family is consciousness. Your friends are consciousness. Your co-workers are consciousness. Everyone is consciousness. While you will recognize each other as a unique extension of consciousness, you're really a collection of consciousness. It is eternal. It is not limited to the body. It is ever-present. It is also an all-knowing consciousness.

Speaking of close and family relationships, have such associations generally known each other in prior incarnations?

Indeed, we have much for you. First off, let's explain to you how you ended up in this human experience. You and everyone else who is in this human experience focused themself into form, focused their consciousness into the human experience, into the exact specifications of when, where, and how they incarnated. You have lived many lives together. You have experienced yourselves together in multiple different dimensions of consciousness. You have been all things to each other. However, it's not really happening in the past like you think of it. It's all happening now. This is just the dimension of consciousness and the experience you're focused in now, so you have more awareness of that person in their specific role—friend, parent, sibling, partner—in this experience that you know as you than the multidimensional nature and your relationship.

You are God, and the other person is God. You are playing in your relationships because you choose to create within these experiences, as the God you are. That's how powerful energy is. That is how powerful consciousness is. You draw yourselves together in form, again and again. You focus yourselves into each other's creations.

HEALTH AND RECOVERY

On the subject of being in form, and more particularly my own, I want to touch on health challenges. About a year and a half ago I found that I have atrial fibrillation, which simply means heart palpitations. The first time it happened, it was pretty scary because I didn't know what was happening. It took six weeks before they shocked it out of me through cardioversion, though it often recurs. Sometimes it'll go away within an hour and sometimes it takes a week. It seems to be tied to stress, though I am not sure. Perhaps it's simply due to an aged body?

No, it's because of your vibration and frequency. You might even recognize yourself that you are living at much higher vibrations and levels of consciousness than ever before. Even your body is in a higher state. So while you think you were under a lot more stress at other times in your life, you were also in a much denser vibration, you were in a much denser physical body, and much more tuned in to the density within the physical experience.

You're elevating your consciousness and awareness such that when you now catch yourself dipping in to a lower vibration, the stress will seem so much greater. You're not anywhere near the levels of stress you used to be in, but stress is going to feel more awful to you now than ever before because you've evolved into these more expanded states of peace, joy, harmony, and well-being and are there for longer periods of time.

Take the perspective or be aware that everything in the physical body is a message for you. It's really your body working on your behalf to communicate with you. It is about having a relationship with your body. Assume or, better said, know that everything is serving in what you want most, which is realization or enlightenment.

If you know that every single thing that's happening in your life is serving in your enlightenment, and your enlightenment is what you want more than anything, then ask the question, "How is this serving in my enlightenment?" We'll tell you it is taking you into an experience where you begin to understand the reason that shocking your heart works is because it evokes a very high frequency into the physical body that allows your heart to recalibrate itself at a steady rate of frequency, to normalize in a higher frequency.

You have the ability to raise your consciousness, which will raise your vibration and your frequency, which would automatically reset your heart. You can do this by coming into a place of stillness, raising your consciousness and your vibration. But most of the time when your heart is beating that fast, it actually triggers a fear-based emotional reaction because you feel like you don't have the ability to come into a place of stillness, or to even have a conscious awareness of the breath. Instead, begin to step back from the one who is experiencing the heart palpitations, and notice that you are the one observing the one that is experiencing the heart palpitations.

As you step back, put some space around yourself and breathe. Within the experience, even though your heart maybe hasn't stopped palpitating, the most important thing for you is to understand that normalization is about coming into an absolute place of stillness within you and that there's nothing more important than that. Not trying to push through it. Not trying to keep getting everything done you think you need to get done. Not trying to figure out what's wrong.

Even the judgment of something being wrong with you creates resistance and a reaction that is taking you out of your conscious state in that moment. It is your conscious state in the moment that will elevate you and your physical body beyond the experience and normalize the systems in your body again. Do you understand?

I do, I do. I think while you're speaking to my health issue, what you're saying will be highly useful for all readers. When I am in a period of atrial fibrillation, it feels like a loss of control, like falling apart. But from what you've said, I understand that I have the ability to detach (to the degree I can) and realize that this is serving me. It's a wake-up call to see things differently, to disentangle and chill out.

Indeed. And so, you are *consciousness*. You are also this *you* that you know as you. You are a field of consciousness, as we have explained. You are focused within the human experience, which means you're also *part* of human consciousness. Even if you have elevated your own consciousness to the highest levels, you're still expressing yourself through the physical body, within the physical experience.

Then, there is a mass consciousness collective. You're also on a planet. The stars and the sun and the moon and the sky and the waves and the nature and the seasons and everything has an impact on each other. It is either working together in your perspective harmoniously, and you're living in a loving, harmonious, supportive world, or you look at what's wrong and the chaos and the trauma and the drama and the suffering, and you live in a hostile, violent, miserable world.

You get to choose how you experience it within your experience. *However, you are still part of this experience and this system that makes up the Earth experience.* For example, when an entire planet in your solar system, like Mercury, goes retrograde, you recognize that there are some effects within the human consciousness and within your own. When the sun shines on the other side of the planet, you recognize that it's dark where you are. You don't try to push against it and try to force the sun to come out at midnight.

You embrace the moonlight. And you recognize that nothing's gone wrong. It's just part of nature and the balance of the sun and the moon and the stars and the orbits and all these things. You can stay conscious and present to these things without pushing against or creating resistance within you.

Most of the time when you get triggered, you look for what has gone wrong or for what you have done wrong, which is always going to entangle you in a lower dimensions of consciousness where there's struggle or an experience of limitation.

If you could see things differently, that it's a sensation that you feel. "Oh, oh, my heart must be speeding up because there's some momentum coming here, and I want to integrate the momentum in my body." In changing your perspective, you elevate yourself out of the resistance you feel. It's like the tension created when pulling a rubber band back, but when you let it go, it flies forward with even more momentum.

If you could see these things happening *for* you, that when these heart palpitations come, it's a sensation preparing for a quantum leap forward, momentum is happening, a huge shift, another level of something really big that's coming. Then all you have to do is ground and integrate and come into even greater harmony, remembering that everything is happening for you.

The message from your body might be that you need greater stillness, even greater presence. Focus on the basics, like your breath. The message from your body might also be to tone down your schedule a bit and come into a time of rest and rejuvenation and integration because there's some huge momentum coming.

Notice, the last time you had an experience like this, that on the other side of it, after you had gone through it, you did experience some great momentum in your life, huge momentum, huge changes.

You might even notice certain patterns, like a Mercury retrograde is coming in to slow things down a bit because it's preparing for a bigger shift that's happening for you.

Stillness is the access point to acceleration. Stillness and presence are the access point to acceleration. Stillness is how your body prepares for acceleration.

Now, is it always going to be this way? No. But we want you to get so comfortable with stillness and slowing down, so totally accepting of it, even appreciating it, that you're not doing anything to try to make it go away. You'll start to catch on to the energetic feeling of being more comfortable with stillness, with presence, with rejuvenation, with times of rest. You'll begin to be in a more natural state of flow instead of trying to do what your human mind always tries to do, which is push through when you feel the resistance. You're trying to push energy where you think it should go instead of just opening and allowing and coming into greater presence and stillness.

Really, truly, just choose to remember that everything in the human experience is serving in your enlightenment, which is why you are here.

This is the incarnation that you and our readers have chosen to come into full realization and live in physical form as fully enlightened masters, not to leave the planet. It is so important, because there's so many in human consciousness who are asking, who know, who remember somewhere within them that the most important thing in this life experience is your own realization. Yet because it doesn't demand of you, it often becomes the thing that is easy to put on the backburner, until it's not.

Your soul, your higher self, your being, has always known that your enlightenment—and realization—was the most important thing. But because your human mind didn't have a perception of it or a perspective of it, there was always so much more that demanded your time. It was your job, all the things that need to get done, your family, your responsibilities that got your attention.

When you come into this place of understanding, from where you are now, that it is coming into these moments of realizing that you are realized. You say "Oh, I just realized something. Oh, I just had an aha moment." That's realization. That's enlightenment. When you're outside and looking at a tree and just in the moment with the tree; you've never really noticed it before, but you have a realization and are, for the first time, really noticing this tree, that's enlightenment. That's realization.

As you start to shift your perspectives because of this new level of awareness, you'll look for the moments within your day when you say, "I just had a realization; I just had a moment of realization." There'll be more moments and more moments until all day long, you are noticing that you are realized within your own experience of realization. You will know that everything is serving in your realization and your enlightenment, and everything will take you into an even deeper state of enlightenment and a deeper state of realization.

So, what's happening on the planet is happening for you. What's going on around you is happening for you. What's going on within you is happening for you. It's all serving in your enlightenment and taking you into deeper levels of your enlightenment.

Then one begins to understand that True Creation is not about getting the perfect parking spot right in front of the building. If the only parking spot you found was a block down the road, you would know that spot was there for a reason. You would know that the whole universe orchestrated that so that you would walk down that block. You would get excited to walk down the block. And while at first there might have only been one reason you were walking down that block, because you are realized and have come into enlightenment, now there's a hundred beautiful things that are reflected to you in that one block.

One of the ways into realization is through seeing all the beauty in everyone and everything. When you no longer see another as separate, you do not see them as broken. Then, you can see the beauty where others cannot. You see the beauty within everyone no matter who or what they appear to be. Do you understand?

Yes, I do.

So, beauty is going to take you all the way into enlightenment, our friend.

Can you please share more on self-realization and enlightenment?

Self-realization is what you are when you're not doing all the other things that keep you from opening and allowing the energy that will serve you that is the frequency of I Am Creator or I am God.

We'll continue to expand on this. The thing that most struggle with—especially ones who've learned to function at very high levels with the analytical and logical mind—is that you habitually go to your brain, to your logical mind for the answers. You cannot find realization through the brain. You cannot find enlightenment through the mental mind.

There is no interest in what is right or what is wrong from the I Am Creator frequency. It is known that all is perfect. When you know yourself as the God that you are, you know you are so much more, and you choose to not to entangle at the price of your frequency with trauma and drama.

Those ready to awaken already have a great deal of compassion. All of the greats, all of the masters, had a great deal of compassion. What happens is when you're seeing another in a lower state of vibration, in a heavy, dense, slower rate of vibration, in the suffering, you judge that as bad and then you dive full in to try to fix it, which entangles you and automatically drags down your vibration. You find yourself in more of a density where instead of feeling all of that openness, all of that knowing, all of that possibility, now you feel constricted because you yourself are now entangled in the density.

Again, be aware of what you're entangling in. Anytime you judge anything, anytime you judge anyone, you entangle with it. Resistance and reaction are always going to stop the flow, this openness and allowing of your energy, your energy, the I Am Creator frequency that is you, to flow in and serve you. Once you move into enlightenment and realization, you know it's all perfect. You are beyond the needing and the wanting. When you go beyond needing and wanting, you will know that you have everything. And in that, there is eternal consciousness.

When you know that you have everything, that's when you can allow yourself into the being state, because in being it is all done through you. In the doing, there's always more to be done. When you come into the I Am Creator frequency and you open and allow, all things are done through you; you move through experience with a knowing. It will feel as if you are sitting in the center of the universe, moving through reality.

That is your force field. The more open and allowing you are, the more frequency and vibration you're allowing through you, the more access to awareness and consciousness that you have, and the more power. The greater your innocence, the more impeccable your power.

It's a dance with creation, with infinite intelligence.

If you just get into that space of allowing, then it'll come. That space of allowing is you allowing infinite intelligence—the consciousness, the awareness that sees the whole picture, that is beyond the limitation of form viewing life through limited senses. It sees everything. It sees every possibility. It sees every potential. And it sees the easiest, most effortless path from where you are to the highest and best good in all situations.

Why wouldn't you allow that? Why wouldn't you want to dance with infinite intelligence, with Source? That is what we refer to as divine orchestration. You learn to allow divine orchestration. Your only job is to get into the energy of allowing the highest and best good.

You, the beautiful, wonderful personality that you know as you doesn't have the whole viewpoint, doesn't know all the possibilities and perspectives that are available here. But if you will open and allow, the solution will always present itself with effortless ease. Open and allow in a vibration of pure love, which we know you all have a great capacity for.

TRUE JOY AND THE KINGDOM OF HEAVEN

Instead of me leading you to my next question, is there anything else that you would like to impart in this precious time we have together?

We want you to always know that we honor the desires of your personality and what it would like to experience. There is never ever a wrong answer or anything that is off path when you are pursuing or experiencing something that is delightful to your personality and to your heart's desires.

The desires of your soul are always for expansion, always expanding through your experiences. There is data and information in any and all experiences. Your soul's desire is for expansion. You are one that will always continue to reach for expansion and want to experience more from expanded levels. The more you expand, the greater awareness you have.

Know that when you have expanded beyond your current physical reality, it begins to feel restrictive, frustrating, exhausting. This happens when you don't allow yourself to go with your expansion. You will find a greater ease and grace in navigating through your own transformation as you allow your consciousness to be the thing that makes the shift. Don't go into the logical mind to try to figure out or make that shift happen. Let your consciousness lead the way.

The second thing we want to say to you is that your soul's desires are also for greater expression, expressing more of who you are, fuller expression of all that you are in physical form. You have been bright, shining lights in many regards. Now, how do you want to more fully express all that you are? Not because that's what other people want from you or what you think they need from you, but because you can finally feel yourself expressing who you really are more fully in every moment of your life experience. That's where you're going next.

The third thing we would say is that your soul's desires are also about experience. What do you *want* to experience? If you can just be aware of these words, "What am I supposed to do?" versus "What do I want to experience?" Know that everything you could ever possibly want and need will be there for you before you even know that you need it.

The more you can practice that on a daily basis—asking, "What do I want to experience today? What is it that I want more of?"—the more you will move into that level of mastery where you begin to understand that you don't get what you want, you don't get what you think you need, you get more of what you are. When you know who you really are, then you can expand and express yourself, knowing that as you move through experience, you will draw things to you from your force field that already exist.

You would no longer ask the question, "What do I want?" You would only ever ask, "What do I want to experience *more* of?" Because from there there's no separation. There's no gap. It's already there. What do you want more of? "I want more freedom, love, abundance, well-being, joy, adventure, passion, inspiration, creativity, beauty, and fun."

Then you begin to expand the field around you, and drawing more of it to you in that field. And so there's no more figuring everything out. There's no more trying to effort and force and make it happen. You move through the world with a level of ease and grace that you've probably seen little to no one ever live in. That is true mastery.

This next phase of your life is living mastery within the human experience before you officially take your seat at the table with the ascended masters, because that is what each of you are. You have full choice over your experience. You choose wherever you want to go from here. This next chapter of your lives is really living what mastery means in the human experience here and now.

Never forget, though: allow your worthiness to be known by you. Are you worthy of it all coming to you with ease? Are you worthy of doing what you love and having everything else figure itself out? Are you worthy of doing what you most enjoy doing, for you? It doesn't matter if anyone else approves or likes it. Know your own worthiness to a level that you can be all that you are. And let it be easy and effortless. Let it come to you without forcing or efforting or figuring it out.

There's no limit. You're going to understand that the currency by which you live is your consciousness. As you step into higher states of consciousness, more and more becomes available to you and things work differently from a higher state of consciousness. Your currency is your consciousness.

You have this. It's opening and allowing. We say this so lovingly to all humans—your addiction to logic is the only thing that keeps it from you. The brain is an incredible machine. It's not who you really are. You never intended to go to the logical mind to help you with presence, with power, with consciousness, with expansion, with expression, with experience. It's an incredible perceiving mechanism. It's an incredible data storage system.

It's an incredible computer that runs all the systems of the body that you would never want to even think about.

Your incredible brain is running your nervous system, your endocrine system, your circulatory system, your reproductive system. It's running all these systems, millions and millions and millions of pieces of data that your brain is managing all day long. Let it do its job.

You're meant to tune in to consciousness for guidance, for the next perfect step. You're meant to tune in, open, and allow yourself to be in your power in the present moment. That is the I Am Presence. That's what you never intended to forget. We certainly understand why you do forget, and that's why the human experiment is such a magnificent one.

Tell me, what do you want more of? Tell me the first thing that comes to mind, what is it?

Supreme peace through understanding the adventure. And the time and space that leads to freedom, that leads to a knowingness that I am in control, that I am the creator, and all is well. I would like enlightenment.

So you say, "I want to experience more enlightenment. I want to feel more enlightenment." This is the process: it can take 10 seconds or a minute or however long, but do it because it feels good. Close your eyes and move from your head down into your heart. This is an important step for you. Close your eyes, get out of your head, move your awareness from your head down into your heart, and feel from within you what enlightenment feels like. What does it feel like? Supreme peace, what does it feel like?

Confidence, joy, love, clarity.

Can you feel it within you? And where do you feel it within you?

I feel it in my heart.

So, feel it. Feel it in your heart, then feel it even deeper, and feel it because it feels really good. Notice, this thing that you're wanting is already within you. You've just got to activate it, which might mean aligning with it. Go into your heart and stay there, and really feel it. Feel it all the way up to the top of your head. Feel it all the way down to the bottom of your feet. Feel it, all the way out from your fingertips if you were to spread them widely. Then direct every cell in your body, coming from your heart, coming from your power center, to align with the feeling of enlightenment.

Feel into that and direct every cell of your body, all the way up from the top of your head to the bottom of your feet and out your fingertips, to align with the frequency, with the feeling of enlightenment, of supreme peace and understanding and joy. Stay there, focusing every single one of your cells, directing them, aligning them to the feeling of enlightenment. Can you feel that?

I think I can, but I feel like the "lid" is not opened yet!

The lid's not on the top, it's inside. That's why you've heard so many times—so many say, it's all within you. It is within you, but you've got to activate it from within. You've got to flip the switch from within. You've got to go within you and find it, feel it, align with it.

You are a feeling being. Beyond anything and everything else, you're a feeling being. You focus through that feeling mechanism. Practice this just a bit, instead of looking out there for enlightenment, instead of searching and seeking out there, go within, go from your head down into your heart, and you will feel what enlightenment feels like.

Maybe at first you just feel it in a couple of cells. Then, next time you find yourself busy and overwhelmed and you ask, "What do I want? What do I want to experience more of?" Enlightenment? Then do the practice we spoke about. Close your eyes. Shift your attention from your head down into your heart; you will instantly feel more alignment with enlightenment, and now there are a few more cells and a few more cells. And you're directing them. You can feel it. They're starting to align with this feeling of enlightenment.

One day you will feel the absolute resonance that every cell of your body is aligned to the frequency of enlightenment. You created it through *feeling* for it and then focusing every cell of your body to align with that feeling that you want more of. Then the next piece from there, once you can direct every cell of your body to align with the frequency and feeling of enlightenment, you'll begin to expand it outwardly to your light, to your force field, and all around you. And by the way, you can do that with any and everything.

When you come across another that you might've wanted to fix or help, now you go, "What do I most want more of in this experience?" Maybe the person is suffering, and you just want them to feel peace. Instead of trying to figure it out for them, you feel peace within yourself, focusing every cell of your body into an alignment with peace. Feel it so deeply that you begin to expand that feeling, that frequency, that vibration, that field of peace that you're creating. It comes from within you. Your light fills the entire space around you, in every direction for as far as you can imagine, coming from within you, infused with the vibration of peace that will be felt all around you. That is how the master of the Self creates the world they want to live in.

From that place, if you were with another or a group of many others who were struggling or suffering, if you were to ask them what they most want, they would say peace. Even if they said money, the reason that they would want money is because they want the struggle to end; ultimately, they want peace.

The only way you can bring peace to the world is through you, through you aligning with it in your own being, directing every cell of your own body into an alignment with peace and then expanding it from there. You get more of what you are, and you learn to expand that within your force field. And then people will say, "I just feel more peaceful when I'm around you. I just feel like everything's going to be okay when I'm around you." It's not because of anything you'd said or anything you did or anything you fixed for them. It's because you did the only thing you really can do to create a better world, which is first create it within you, or better said, align with it or activate it from within you. You understand?

The Kingdom of Heaven lies within.

What is in the Kingdom of Heaven? Peace, joy, harmony, bliss, love, connection, companionship, health, well-being, abundance, freedom. All of it. Beauty. You can't imagine the beauty that's here for you, just waiting to be activated by you.

We know we have brought a great deal of information to you. Yet, we tell you and our readers that you are the ones who drew this to you. You really are the ones who channeled this to you. It is your asking. It is already in your consciousness. It is already in your awareness. You drew to yourselves the experience of all that you already know.

This has been so powerful.

Indeed, our friend. We tell you that the most important of our teachings is that everything you wish to be, you already are. It is all within you. It always has been. It always will be.

If you are in the lack and limitation and not feeling the peace, the joy, the freedom, the love, the abundance, and the well-being, it's because you are keeping yourself from these kinds of experiences. In lower dimensions of consciousness, you are perceiving lack and, therefore, still needing and wanting something outside of you, creating a resistance that will not allow you to access the magic and miracles.

Our intention is not to create further distractions that cause you to deny your own joy, peace, freedom, love, abundance, and well-being. There is already so much distraction in the human experience that causes you to put your focus on things outside of yourself, because you think they are affecting your ability to create your own reality. You start believing that everything is happening *to* you, which only perpetuates a sense of powerlessness.

We are here to remind you that joy, peace, love, harmony, freedom, well-being, and abundance are the reasons why you are here. You're here to embody, create, align, and live with them; they are your true nature. All of it is within you; therefore infuse your creations and manifestations with their fullness.

I see. There's no human need to create miracles or perform mind-blowing feats to prove anything; it's about our joy. Your answers have guided us in this direction throughout the book, and it's been beautiful.

There will be so many miracles. Every day will shower you with miracles when you're living at this level.

You will be in joy and peace and love and harmony and in the state of freedom and well-being and abundance—so whole and complete within yourself and so satiated by every moment, yet still you'll continue drawing more and more of these things to you. Source, God, Creator will unendingly orchestrate manifestations of magic and miracles.

And, indeed, perceiving into potentials and possibilities and celebrating your gifts and talents is a wonderful part of all of this. It will come to you. But for now, what you are seeking will bring about the highest wisdom in service to the highest good for humanity, which is for everyone to realize that they have the power within themselves to create their own experience.

Will you always continue to explore other realms of potentials and possibilities? Indeed. But you will do this from the vibration, the level of consciousness, of being whole and complete and full and filled up and satiated—where you're not needing and you're not wanting. When you are not in lack, when you are not in limitation, when you are not experiencing fear, and when you are not experiencing separation, all your power will be revealed to you.

As easy and effortless as this all sounds—and will one day be—for me and countless others, I wonder why more people, kids in their joy or adults in their wisdom, don't sometimes experience spontaneous or full-blown enlightenment?

You all begin your lives as pure Source energy. A child is naturally very joyful and enlightened in themselves. They're spontaneous and feel a powerful sense of freedom and joy and love and well-being. Yet very quickly they're immersed in the perceptions and beliefs of others: "Oh, that's not safe. You've got to get this done. You've got to go to school. You've got to get up. You've got to wear this. You've got to stop doing that, and shouldn't do that, and stop talking, and don't speak like that."

When your physical senses are inundated so strongly with data that you are not the pure bliss that you have felt yourself to be, you begin to perceive yourself in limitation. There are those, however, when not in resistance, at any age, who do have those spontaneous experiences and remember, "I am not these limitations that I learned to be." Does that make sense?

I would still think that at least one out of a million children would not be so tamped down by well-meaning adults that they would suddenly be in a state of enlightenment.

But many children are!

They are?

Indeed. And how would you know that they were in that state?

Well, they would be living in such joy, and they would find life so effortless; everything would come easily, and they would attract more and more knowledge of their true nature and be able to see through the illusions that everybody else bought into. They would be the light, saying things like, "Hey, look at what I'm doing; you can do this too!" And some might even become teachers.

You've got it, our friend. We are finding such complete and total joy in the irony of what you just said. As you have just described yourself, and yet you can't even see it. You were talking about an enlightened being, yet you don't consider yourself one of them. But you are.

Well, I do see some irony there.

This will help you. Indeed, as the vibration and the consciousness of humanity continues to elevate and expand, you're going to see more and more people around you that are joyful, happy, free, peaceful, abundant, and experiencing well-being.

You are in the human experience. Most of you are still very much entangled in the mass-conscious collective, perceiving yourselves in a very human way. There is nothing wrong with this; it is part of the journey through different levels of consciousness.

Imagine a child that is raised outside of the mass-conscious, collective experience. Perhaps they are homeschooled, don't watch TV, and have highly conscious, joyful, loving parents. Most of that child's experience is playing in nature and teaching their parents about what they're learning, instead of the parents teaching the children. The parents encourage their child to explore their imagination and play and create and laugh and have fun with their friends. Chances are you would find that child to be much more "high vibration." The reason for this is that they are still connected to their true nature.

When a child is focused primarily in the collective experience, and they get up, go to school, and do their homework every day at around the same time, and they watch TV and movies, and participate in popular culture, social media, and all these things, you're going to find that they perceive themself much more within that collective experience than in elevated states.

We're not saying to reject all those things. However, it does, again, relate to why there are so many stories of people in your culture going out into the desert, or into the forest, or to the top of the mountain with the desire and intent to tune in to themselves and get clear. They are all searching for the same thing—a connection to Source, to the pure Source energy that they are. They want to know who they are and to realize that at such a deep level it would never matter again where they focused themselves, because they would never forget the joy, the peace, the love, the freedom, the abundance, and the well-being that they truly are.

Yes. And as you've said, the energies on the planet are shifting; we are at higher levels of consciousness than ever before, meaning that our manifestations can be realized more quickly than ever before.

Indeed. You are entering into the most powerful times of your life. You are no longer preparing. You are no longer an initiate. You are masters. And we have said now is the time. We have said this is what you've been waiting for and preparing for. And we really mean that; this is it. This is what you came for. This is why you are here.

This time on your planet is bringing forth the greatest, most expansive wave of awakening that has ever occurred. You are going to see the greatest wave of awakening humanity has ever experienced. You're going to see it all around you. You're going to see it in your friendships, in your relationships, in your co-workers, with strangers, and most especially with the people that you likely doubted would ever awaken. They're awakening because of you, because you raised the consciousness, because you raised the vibration, because you brought the light, because you had the courage and the strength and the commitment to fully awaken, to come into realization, and to live as the embodied, enlightened masters that you are.

CONCLUSION

The Great Awakening is here, and it's now, and there's no turning back. It is going to send a wave through every corner of this Earth and this planet. You are needed now more than ever to be all that you are and to live your life fully and to love fully.

We will leave each and every one of our readers with these words:

You've got this.

You don't have to wait anymore for anything else. Just open to and allow all that you are. Keep letting it in. At some point, very soon, you're going to have a moment where you will see it all so very clearly. You are going to say, "I've got this. Oh, now I've got this. I get it. Wow, I made it so much more difficult than it needed to be." And you will smile, knowing that it was all perfect.

We are here on our side because we promised we would be so that you would never forget the truth within you. We have shared a great amount of information with you, and there is so much more to come. We remind you that you are everything you wish to be.

We are always with you. We are always available to you. We love you, we love you, we love you. And with that, we are complete.

ABOUT THE AUTHORS

SARA LANDON is a globally celebrated transformational leader, visionary entrepreneur, and author of *The Wisdom of The Council*. She is the channel of The Council, a collective of ascended master beings with a higher level of consciousness and a grander perspective of the human experience.

MIKE DOOLEY is a *New York Times* best-selling author, metaphysical teacher, and creator of the popular Notes from the Universe, whose acclaimed books—including *Infinite Possibilities* and *The Top Ten Things Dead People Want to Tell You*—have been published worldwide in 27 languages. He was one of the featured teachers in the phenomenon *The Secret* and has presented to live audiences in 156 cities across 42 countries.

Hay House Titles of Related Interest

YOU CAN HEAL YOUR LIFE, the movie,
starring Louise Hay & Friends
(available as an online streaming video)
www.hayhouse.com/louise-movie

THE SHIFT, the movie,
starring Dr. Wayne W. Dyer
(available as an online streaming video)
www.hayhouse.com/the-shift-movie

ASK AND IT IS GIVEN: Learning to Manifest Your Desires, by Esther and Jerry Hicks

THE LAW OF ATTRACTION: The Basics of the Teachings of Abraham by Esther and Jerry Hicks

SOUL LESSONS AND SOUL PURPOSE: A Channeled Guide to Why You Are Here by Sonia Choquette

DIVINE MASTERS, ANCIENT WISDOM: Activations to Connect with Universal Spiritual Guides by Kyle Gray

ORACLE OF THE 7 ENERGIES: A 49-Card Deck and Guidebook

All of the above are available at your local bookstore, or may be ordered by contacting Hay House (see next page).

We hope you enjoyed this Hay House book. If you'd like to receive our online catalog featuring additional information on Hay House books and products, or if you'd like to find out more about the Hay Foundation, please contact:

Hay House, Inc., P.O. Box 5100, Carlsbad, CA 92018-5100
(760) 431-7695 or (800) 654-5126
(760) 431-6948 (fax) or (800) 650-5115 (fax)
www.hayhouse.com® • www.hayfoundation.org

Published in Australia by: Hay House Australia Pty. Ltd.
18/36 Ralph St., Alexandria NSW 2015
Phone: 612-9669-4299 • Fax: 612-9669-4144
www.hayhouse.com.au

Published in the United Kingdom by: Hay House UK, Ltd.
The Sixth Floor, Watson House, 54 Baker Street, London W1U 7BU
Phone: +44 (0)20 3927 7290 • Fax: +44 (0)20 3927 7291
www.hayhouse.co.uk

Published in India by: Hay House Publishers India
Muskaan Complex, Plot No. 3, B-2, Vasant Kunj, New Delhi 110 070
Phone: 91-11-4176-1620
www.hayhouse.co.in